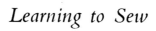

Learning to Sew

Barbara Snook

Learning to Sew

DRYAD PRESS LTD

LONDON

Barbara Snook 1962, 1985
First published in 1962 by B.T. Batsford
This edition published 1985 by Dryad Press Ltd,
London

ISBN 0 8521 9613 X

Printed and bound in Great Britain by
Butler & Tanner Ltd,
Frome and London
for the Publisher
Dryad Press Ltd
4 Fitzhardinge Street
London W1H 0AH

Contents

Introduction

This book is written for all those with little experience in embroidery and needlework, giving equal emphasis to design and construction in the belief that they are equally important. It was intended originally for 9–12-year-olds for whom simplified pages have been inset. Young children have in the past produced beautiful and sometimes intricate work; there is little reason why we today cannot expect a higher standard, even if we do not aspire to that of the first Elizabethan Age.

Embroidery is a craft, therefore we must know how tools and materials can be used to make things strong and beautiful. Somewhere in the book can be found every process that is needed for the many useful things that are illustrated.

Part I is concerned with the essential processes of simple needlework, with equipment, threads and stitches. The use of all these will gradually be learnt and with increasing experience a suitable choice can be made for a piece of work.

Part II briefly explains the development of simple designs and will help in the creation of new ideas; try not to copy exactly any of the motifs in the book, for it is more interesting to alter them until they have gained a new individuality. Although some of the designs in Part III look difficult they are all made from simple shapes. Look carefully at pages 20 and 21 for these will help you to understand how the later designs are constructed.

Part III gives working diagrams of a variety of useful things. Exact sizes are mentioned only for a few standard baby clothes. Designs are not actual size for results will always depend on the choice of fabric and thread.

Only very simple paper patterns are needed.

From the beginning take great care over each process, marking the pattern or pinning it on, cutting out with smooth edges, turning hems, tacking evenly and keeping work clean. When embroidery has to be unpicked the material does not look fresh. Finished work should be ironed carefully, on the wrong side to bring up the embroidery.

One word of warning to young needlewomen; small objects are often much harder to make than large ones . . . the baby shoes on page 104 demand very nimble fingers.

PART I

A Work-box

should contain different kinds of needles and a needle-book, pins and a pin-cushion, sharp scissors, a thimble, inch-tape, tacking and sewing cottons, embroidery threads, press-studs, hooks and eyes, tape, elastic, buttons and a small box for beads and sequins.

A thin piece of card, notched as required, makes an accurate measure.

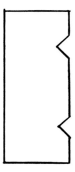

You will also need drawing paper, pencils, wax crayons, and a ruler for use on paper (but not on fabric because its edge is seldom clean, it is too short, and it does not "give" with the fabric).

A Piece-box

is also essential. Try to find a large shallow box for scrap pieces of material; keep them smooth, ready for use. The larger your collection of different kinds of fabric the better, for there will be more to choose from when you begin to make the patchwork cot cover (p. 64), or the appliqué cushion (p. 52) or if the pieces are big enough, the cat cushion (p. 28).

Needles

It is important to choose the correct needle. The eye must make a large enough hole in the fabric for the thread to pass through easily. If it has to be tugged through sharply the eye may break or the thread may be spoilt.
Several different needles are shown on page 14.

Here are their main uses:

Primary, 1, 3, 5	for many different threads.
Sharps 8	for sewing cotton, Sylko, or a single strand of stranded cotton.
Crewel 7	for coton à broder, and 2 or 3 threads of stranded cotton.
Crewel 5	for more than 3 strands of cotton and 2-ply wool.
Chenille, large eye and sharp point	Anchor flox, Anchor soft, tapestry, crewel and 3-ply wool.
Tapestry, large eye and blunt point	for use on canvas, loosely woven fabric, and willow cross stitch fabric.

Special needles are obtainable for Fresca and Perlita.

SEAMS

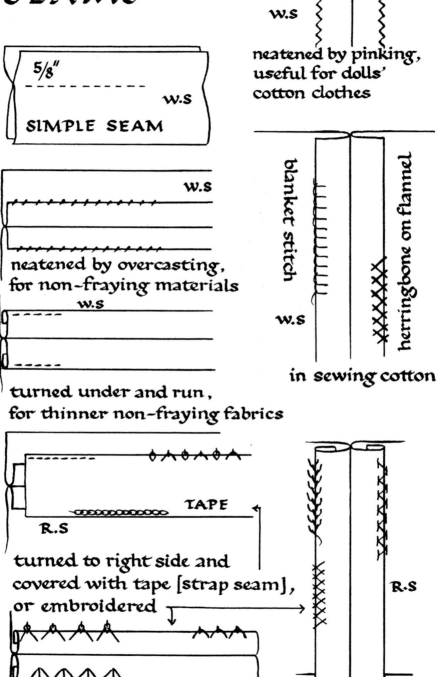

5/8"

w.s

SIMPLE SEAM

w.s

neatened by pinking,
useful for dolls'
cotton clothes

w.s

neatened by overcasting,
for non-fraying materials

w.s

turned under and run,
for thinner non-fraying fabrics

blanket stitch

herringbone on flannel

w.s

in sewing cotton

TAPE

R.S

turned to right side and
covered with tape [strap seam],
or embroidered

R.S

R·S

Do not use all these stitches at once

FRENCH SEAM

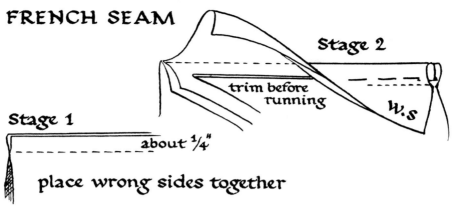

Stage 2

trim before running

w.s

Stage 1

about ¼"

place wrong sides together

RUN AND FELL SEAM

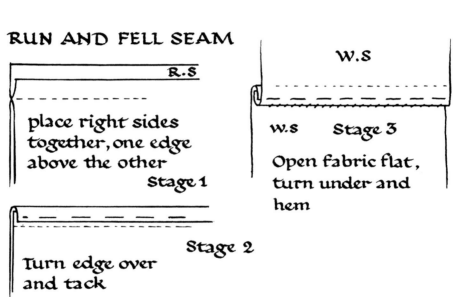

R.S

place right sides together, one edge above the other

Stage 1

W.S

w.s **Stage 3**

Open fabric flat, turn under and hem

Turn edge over and tack

Stage 2

HOW TO TURN DIFFERENT WIDTH HEMS

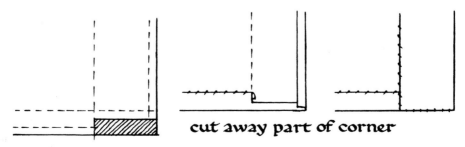

cut away part of corner

NEEDLEWORK STITCHES

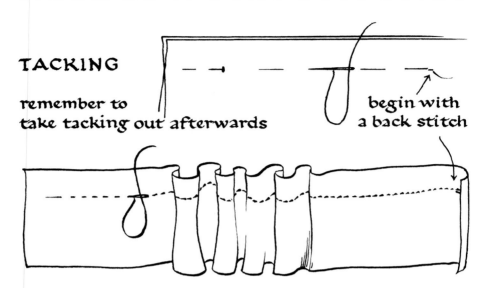

TACKING

remember to
take tacking out afterwards

begin with
a back stitch

RUNNING is used for gathers

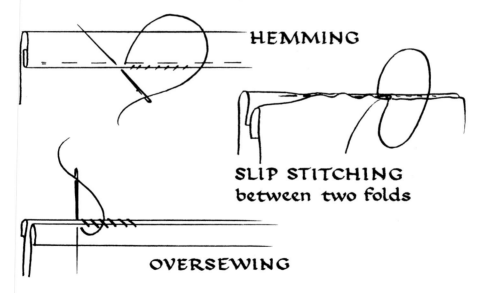

HEMMING

SLIP STITCHING
between two folds

OVERSEWING

this has a straight stitch
on the right side

BIAS BINDING

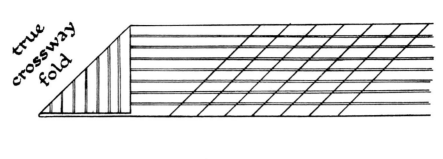

true crossway fold

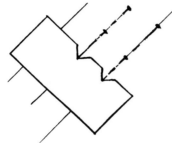

Cut strips the same width using a cardboard measure

Place together for length; each strip is to be as long as possible

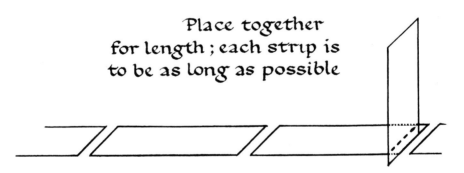

R·S   w.s   RS   RS   cut off

NEEDLES AND THREADS

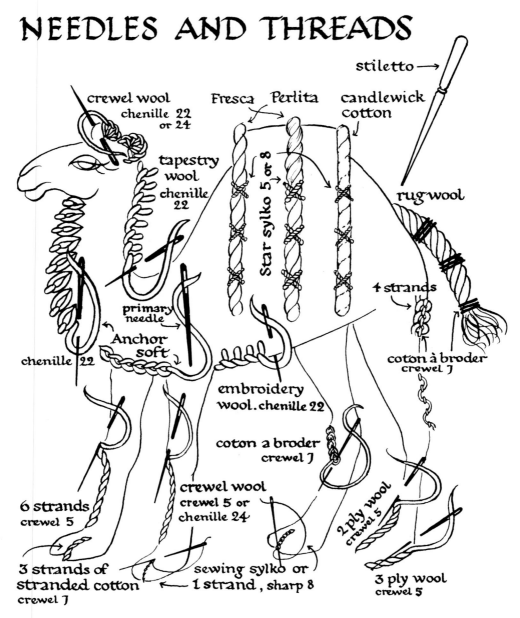

stiletto →

crewel wool
chenille 22
or 24

Fresca Perlita candlewick
cotton

tapestry
wool
chenille
22

Star sylko 5 or 8

rug wool

primary
needle

4 strands

Anchor
soft

chenille 22

coton à broder
crewel J

embroidery
wool. chenille 22

coton a broder
crewel J

6 strands
crewel 5

crewel wool
crewel 5 or
chenille 24

2 ply wool
crewel 5

3 strands of
stranded cotton
crewel J

sewing sylko or
← 1 strand, sharp 8

3 ply wool
crewel 5

Use a stiletto to help very thick threads
through the material

Sometimes a stitch looks better when it is
worked in a certain direction; you will
need to turn the cowboy upside down to
see how some of the stitches are worked

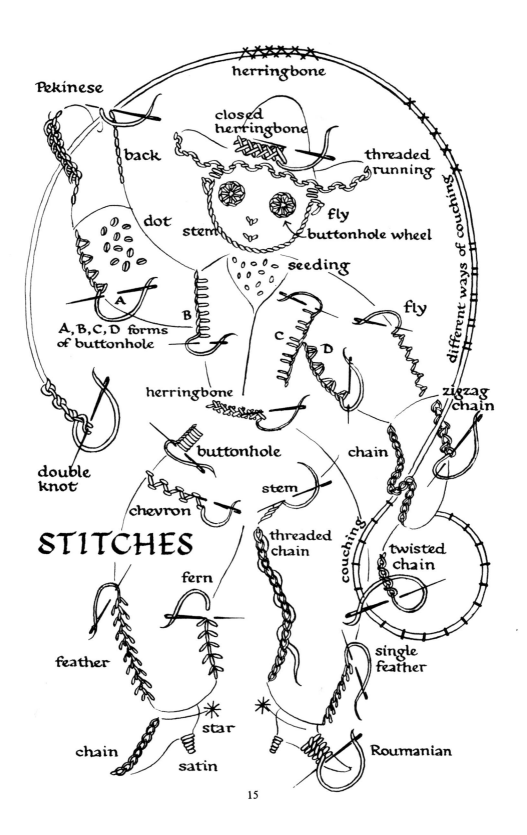

herringbone

Pekinese

closed
herringbone

threaded
running

back

dot

fly

stem

buttonhole wheel

seeding

different ways of couching

A

B

A,B,C,D forms
of buttonhole

C

D

fly

herringbone

zigzag
chain

double
knot

buttonhole

chain

stem

chevron

STITCHES

twisted
chain

couching

threaded
chain

fern

single
feather

feather

star

chain

Roumanian

satin

15

PART II

Pattern

A pattern needs variety.

The pattern A has variety in shape and B has variety in size. A also has contrast in tone

A   B

Tone is a word used to describe dark and light; black and white are the extremes. If all colours in a pattern are the same strength we say they are the same tone. A bold pattern will have contrast in tone.

Panther and tiger show contrast between plain and pattern

Elephant and giraffe show contrast between dark and light, plain and pattern, tall and short

Pig and lamb show contrast between solid mass and line. Many other contrasts can be found in nature, for example, a conker is smooth inside a prickly case

There are other contrasts between smooth and rough, bright and dull, thick and thin.

We are going to use material and thread; silk and satin are bright, flannel has a dull surface; cotton and linen are smooth, tweed is rough; felt is thick, while muslin, net and organdie are thin.

We can choose thick or thin threads such as Anchor soft (thick) and stranded cotton (thin), or bright (Perlita) and dull (wool). These may sometimes be used in the same piece of work.

Look again at the camel on page 14 to find other contrasts.

Colour is very important

Sometimes only one colour will be needed, perhaps matching the fabric, with threads in several tones and thicknesses. On other work many bright colours may be more effective, but there must always be a dark and a light tone amongst them, and one colour must be more important than the rest.

Make experiments with pieces of coloured fabric and strands of different threads; arrange them on a piece of paper; move them around and notice how the effect will change if the amount of each colour is altered.

Another way to experiment is to take a long strip of fabric and pin on it strands of wool and cotton placing them in groups, each representing a colour scheme.

PATTERNS made from
things we see

These PATTERNS show how to
use contrast in tone, size and shape

  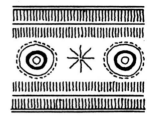

 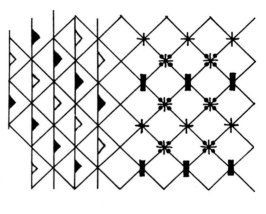

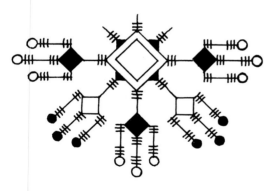 

Variation can
be increased by
the use of thick
and thin thread

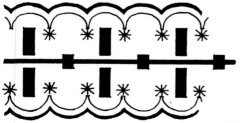 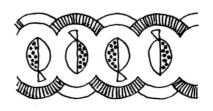

and these diagrams show how some of
them can be embroidered

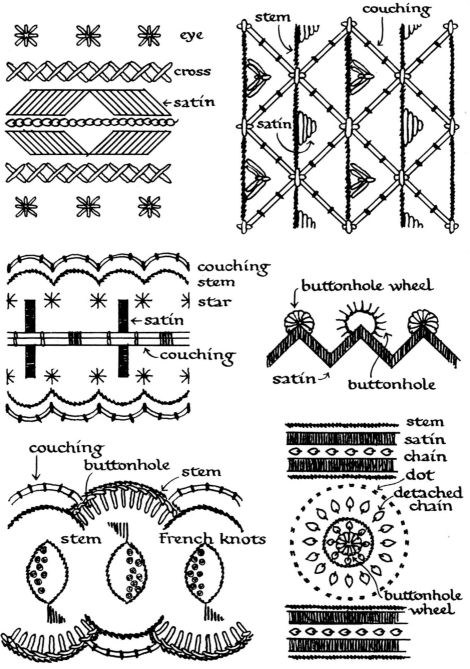

eye

cross

←satin

couching
stem

satin

couching
stem
star

←satin

↖couching

buttonhole wheel

satin↗   buttonhole

couching
buttonhole   stem

stem   French knots

stem   satin
              chain
              dot
              detached
              chain

buttonhole
wheel

PART III

MAT

On coarse
even-weave
fabric or
Cedar cloth

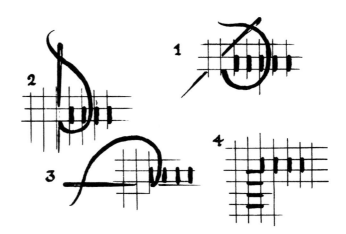

find centre thread

cross stitch

1   2

MAT

Winchester, Holyrood or Windsor cloth

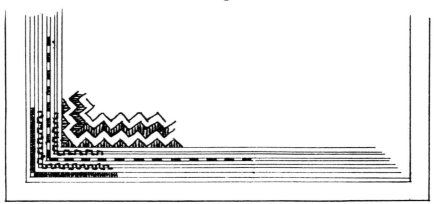

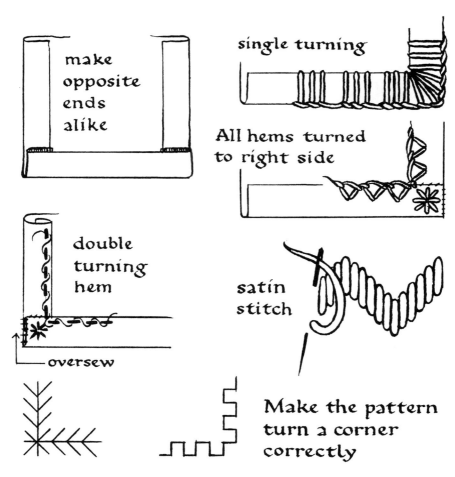

make
opposite
ends
alike

single turning

All hems turned
to right side

double
turning
hem

satin
stitch

oversew

Make the pattern
turn a corner
correctly

25

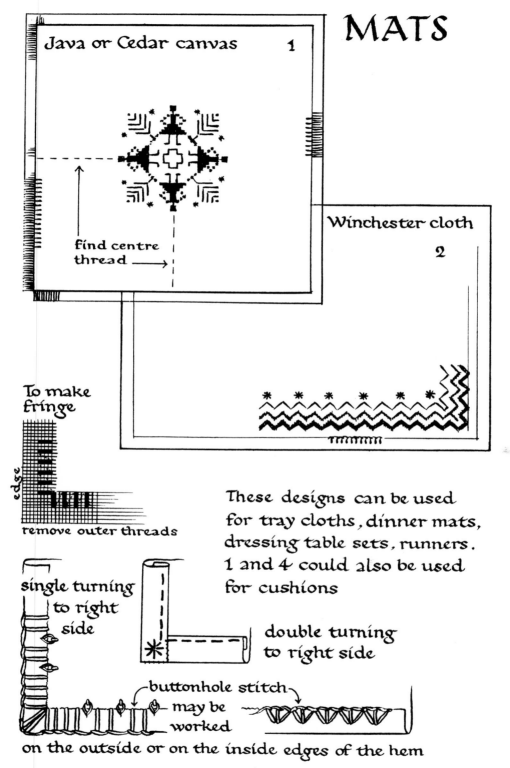

MATS

Java or Cedar canvas   **1**

find centre thread ⟶

Winchester cloth   **2**

To make fringe

edge

remove outer threads

These designs can be used for tray cloths, dinner mats, dressing table sets, runners. 1 and 4 could also be used for cushions

single turning to right side

double turning to right side

buttonhole stitch may be worked on the outside or on the inside edges of the hem

26

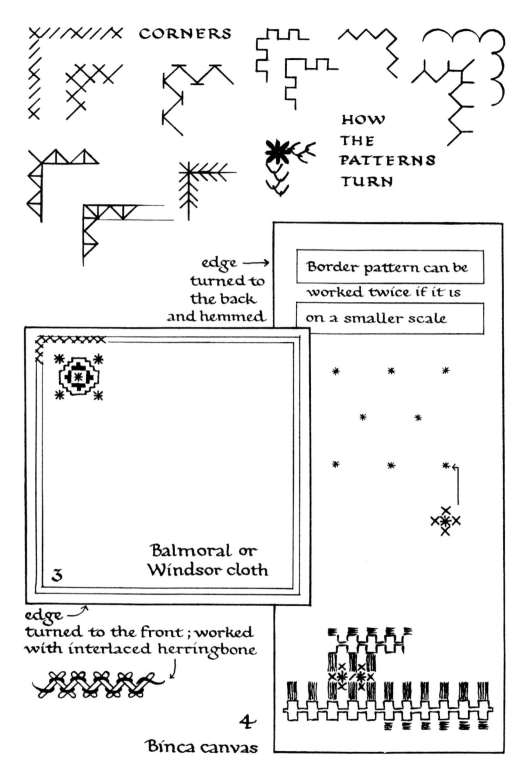

CORNERS

HOW
THE
PATTERNS
TURN

edge →
turned to
the back
and hemmed

Border pattern can be
worked twice if it is
on a smaller scale

3

Balmoral or
Windsor cloth

edge ↗
turned to the front; worked
with interlaced herringbone

4

Binca canvas

CUSHION COVER

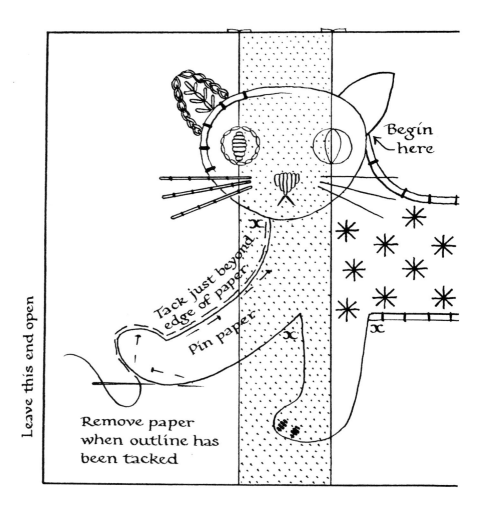

Begin
here

Tack just beyond
edge of paper

Pin paper

Leave this end open

Remove paper
when outline has
been tacked

To make up the cushion place back and
front with right sides together; join with
a simple seam by machine or running
Leave one end open; neaten raw edges
with bias binding or make a narrow hem;
oversew when the cushion is inside

Work on flannel, hessian, Slavonic cloth,
cotton or linen

Join different fabrics with a simple seam

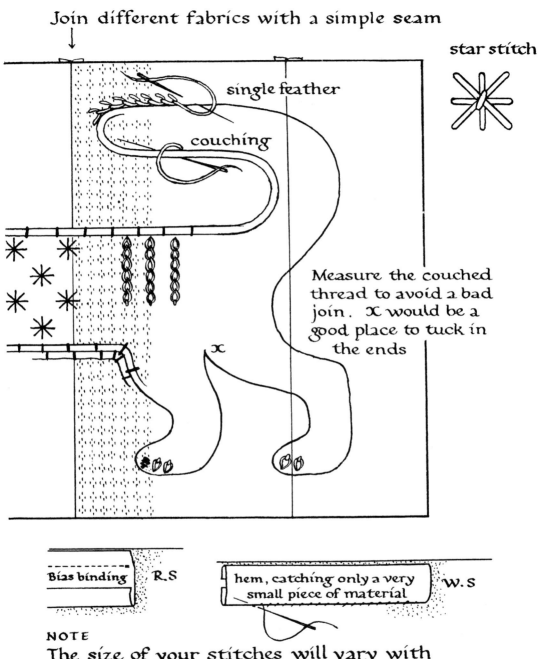

star stitch

single feather

couching

Measure the couched thread to avoid a bad join. x would be a good place to tuck in the ends

Bias binding · R.S

hem, catching only a very small piece of material · W.S

NOTE

The size of your stitches will vary with different thicknesses of thread; more than one row will be needed for all outlines
Use Fresca, Anchor soft and wool

HOUSEWIFE linen lined with
striped cotton or winceyette

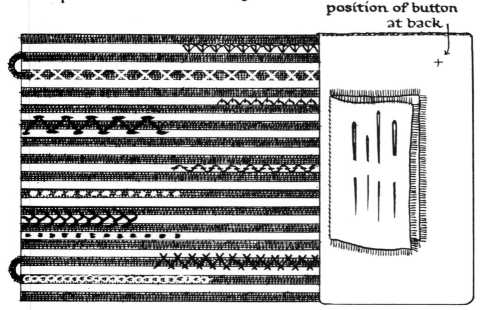

position of button at back

Embroider in grey, white and a darker shade
than the stripes. Line with a matching colour,
placing right sides together

leave opening

Turn to right
side ; slip
stitch together

Fold end over to form pocket
Join seam with faggot stitch

slip stitch

Hem stitch a piece of flannel ; fold it in two
and hem to pocket

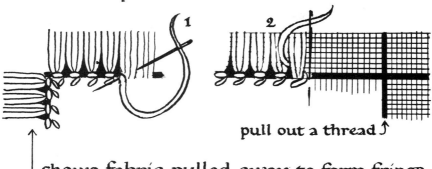

pull out a thread ↥

shows fabric pulled away to form fringe

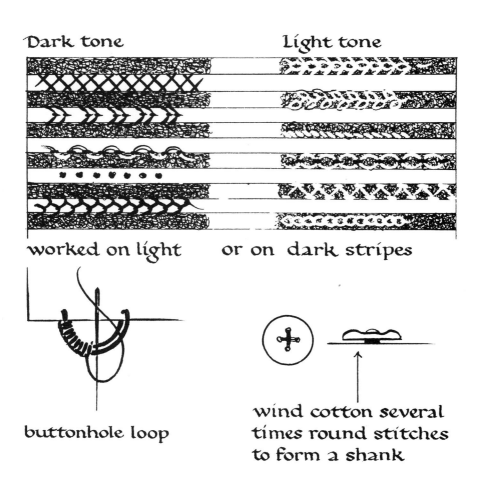

Dark tone   Light tone

worked on light   or on dark stripes

buttonhole loop

wind cotton several
times round stitches
to form a shank

CASE for serviette, gloves or handkerchiefs

Use linen or Slavonic cloth

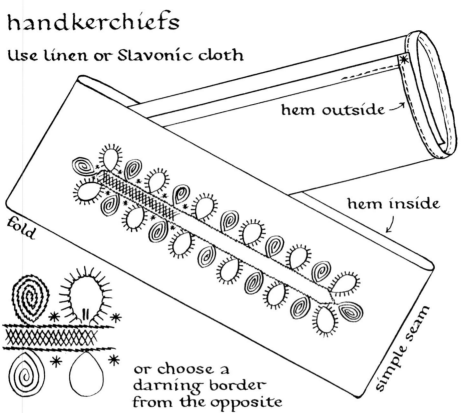

hem outside →

hem inside ↙

fold

simple seam

or choose a darning border from the opposite

HOUSEWIFE

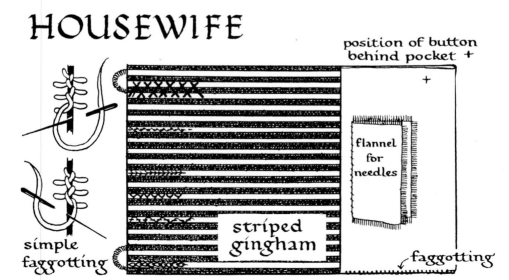

position of button behind pocket +

flannel for needles

striped gingham

simple faggotting

faggotting

for pencils, comb or scissors

felt

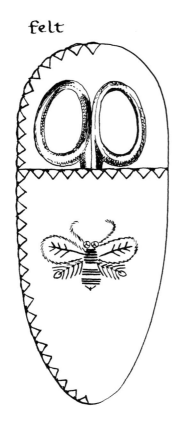

Linen or Willow

Position of closed flap

appearance of double overcasting

Darning borders
for serviette case
or housewife

method

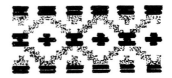

SERVIETTE RING

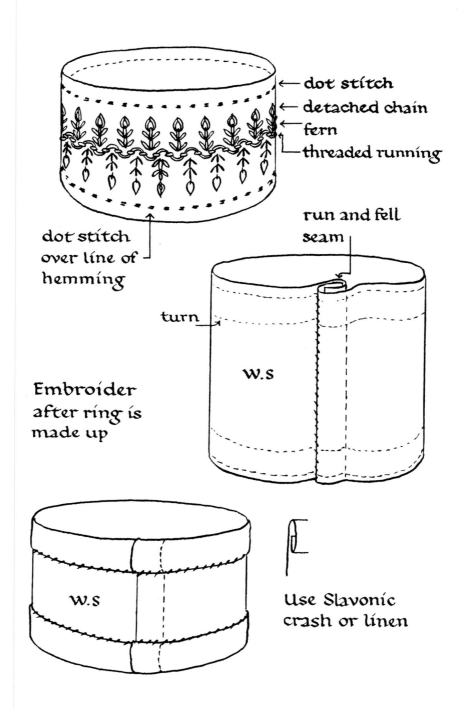

← dot stitch
← detached chain
← fern
← threaded running

dot stitch
over line of
hemming

Embroider
after ring is
made up

run and fell
seam

turn

w.s

w.s

Use Slavonic
crash or linen

PINCUSHION

Use felt and an even-weave fabric

double running

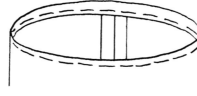

turn edge in once; tack before sewing in the felt circle

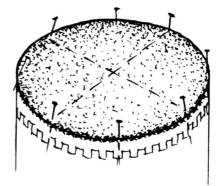

at this point turn and go back to the beginning, filling in gaps

begin

Pin on opposite sides before double overcasting

SERVIETTE RINGS

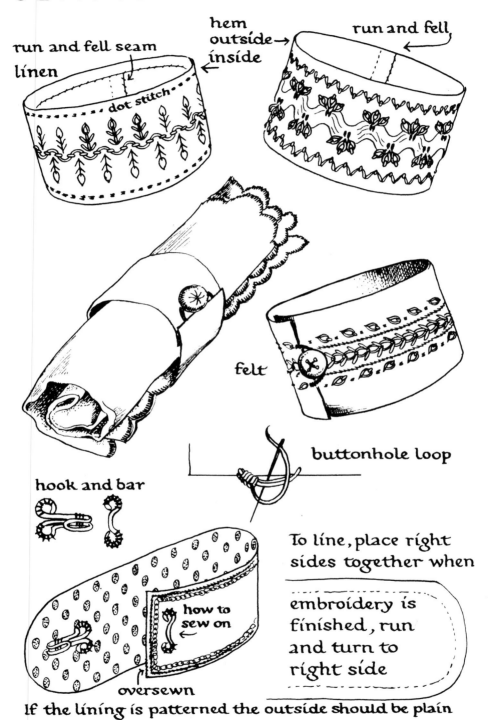

run and fell seam
linen

hem
outside→
inside

run and fell

dot stitch

felt

buttonhole loop

hook and bar

how to
sew on

oversewn

To line, place right
sides together when

embroidery is
finished, run
and turn to
right side

If the lining is patterned the outside should be plain

SPECTACLE CASE

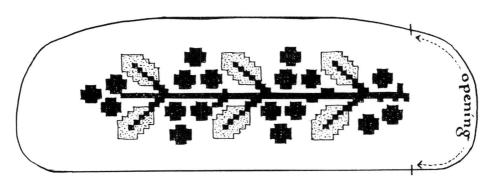

Cut 4 pieces of buckram
exactly the size of the
finished case.

Cover 2 with lining by pasting
down the edges.

Cover the other 2 when embroidery
is finished.

Paste together in pairs,
press until dry.

Oversew each pair separately, catching only
the edge of the fabric.

Finally join both together with double overcast.
Leave one end open

Use an even weave fabric

1   2

cross stitch

BEACH BAG

cord join
hidden
under felt

single seam on selvedge

Made with Turkish towelling, worked with
couched rug wool, Fresca or candlewick cotton,
Anchor soft and coton à broder.
Openings for the cords
are left in the single
seams which have
the selvedge

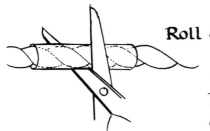

Roll cellotape round cord before it is cut, to prevent ends unravelling.
Bind tightly with embroidery thread.
Fluff out ends

DRAWSTRING METHOD

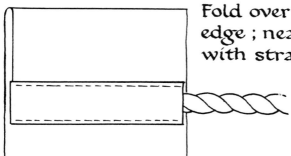

Fold over top edge ; neaten with straight binding through which cords will pass

OTHER METHODS FOR CORD

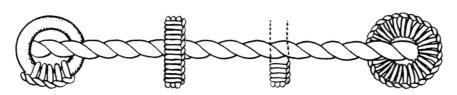

bone ring   buttonhole bars   eyelet

TASSELS

felt

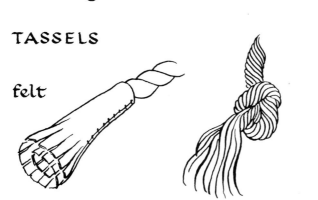

cord taken round toggle and the end

bound to cord

APRON

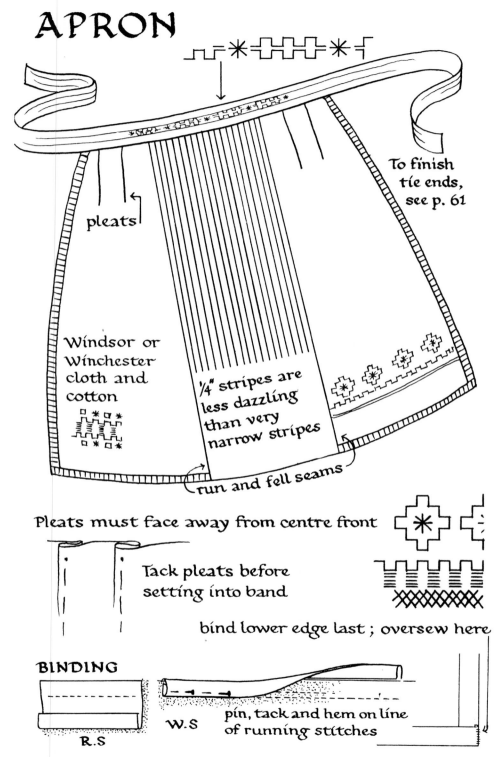

pleats

To finish
tie ends,
see p. 61

Windsor or
Winchester
cloth and
cotton

¼" stripes are
less dazzling
than very
narrow stripes

run and fell seams

Pleats must face away from centre front

Tack pleats before
setting into band

bind lower edge last ; oversew here

BINDING

R.S

W.S

pin, tack and hem on line
of running stitches

40

Setting gathers into a waistband

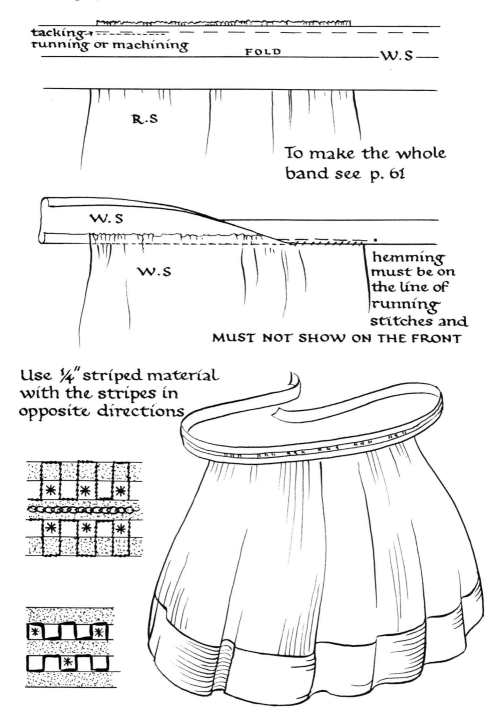

tacking→
running or machining
FOLD
W.S

R.S

To make the whole
band see p. 61

W.S

W.S

hemming
must be on
the line of
running
stitches and
MUST NOT SHOW ON THE FRONT

Use ¼" striped material
with the stripes in
opposite directions

TABLE CLOTH
of 1" square gingham

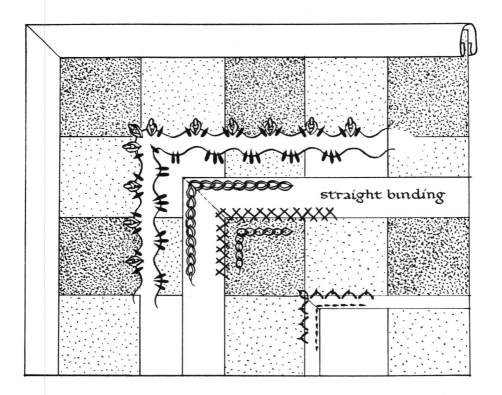

straight binding

How to bind the outside edge

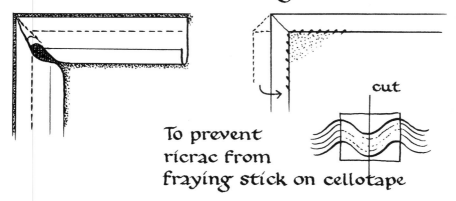

cut

To prevent
ricrac from
fraying stick on cellotape

How to turn straight binding

←cut

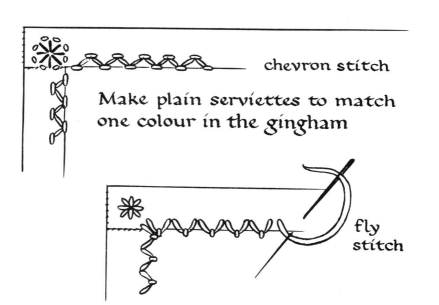

chevron stitch

Make plain serviettes to match
one colour in the gingham

fly
stitch

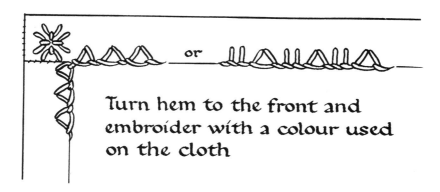

or

Turn hem to the front and
embroider with a colour used
on the cloth

TABLE CLOTH

To mitre this corner with binding see opposite page

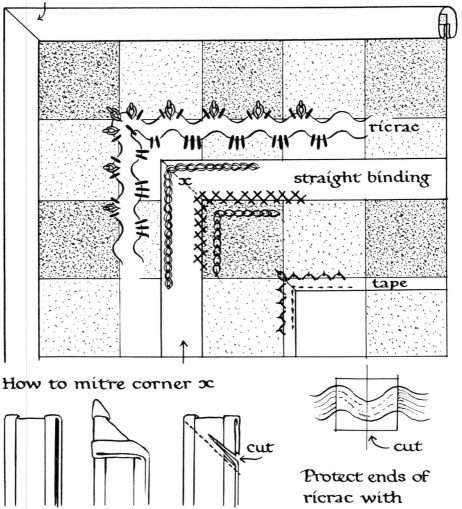

ricrac

straight binding

x

tape

How to mitre corner x

cut

fold binding; turn over corner
and crease; sew along crease;
cut off corner

cut

Protect ends of
ricrac with
cellotape; trim
it away before
joining with
small stitches

Make plain serviettes to match one colour in
the gingham

HARDANGER MAT

Use Aïda or Balmoral canvas for a first attempt

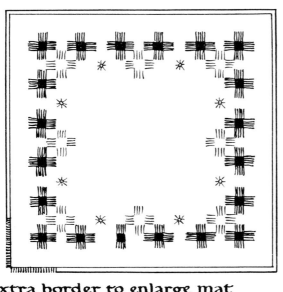

In Hardanger work a hole may be cut only if the raw edge is covered with satin stitch, 5 stitches over 4 threads

extra border to enlarge mat

double running

2 rows double running

To mitre a corner with a bound edge

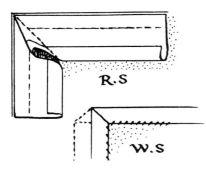

R.S

W.S

The corner must be turned sharply with a 45° fold

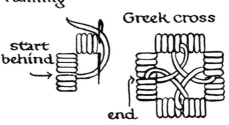

Greek cross

start behind →

end

Experiment with these motifs

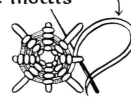

Back-stitched spider web

45

TEA COSY

eye and beak applied felt

oversew felt

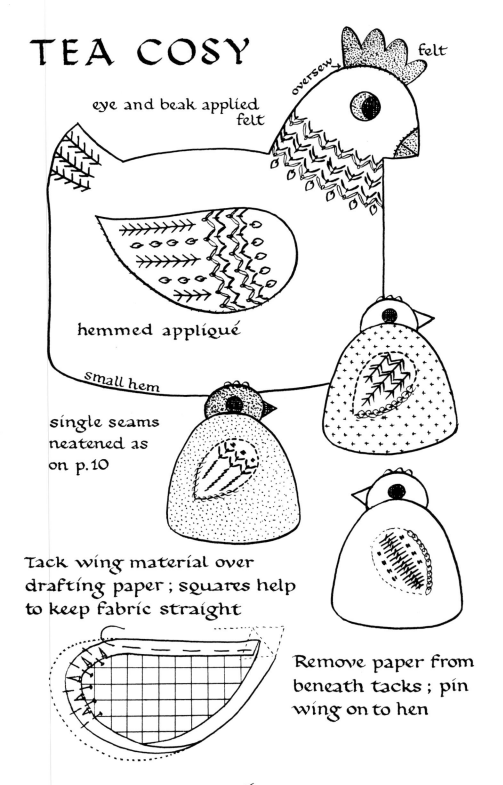

hemmed appliqué

small hem

single seams
neatened as
on p.10

Tack wing material over
drafting paper ; squares help
to keep fabric straight

Remove paper from
beneath tacks ; pin
wing on to hen

46

Make each chick a different colour, using
fabric to match colours of embroidery thread
Use linen, poplin or Oregon cloth

Felt head set in seam
Leave open A-B ; slip head inside ; hem both
sides of cosy to the felt

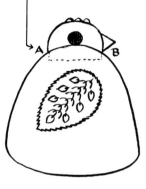

small hem

EGG COSIES

Each chick
has a felt
lining joined
with
antique
seam

another
idea
for a
tea cosy

47

GUEST TOWEL

Work with stranded cotton or coton à broder
on linen

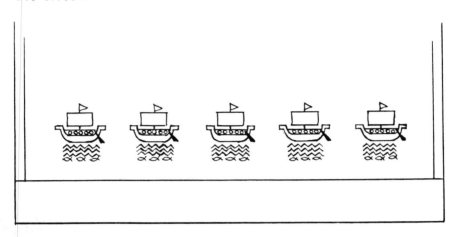

How to turn a corner with different width
hems

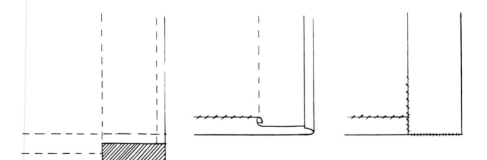

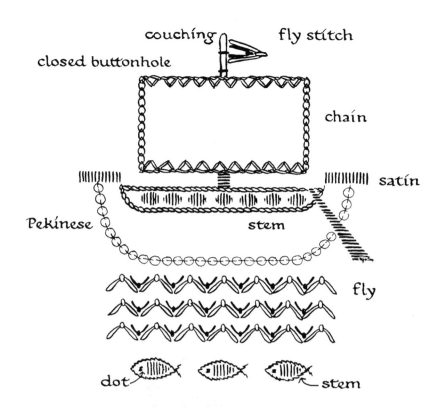

couching fly stitch

closed buttonhole

chain

satin

Pekinese

stem

fly

dot stem

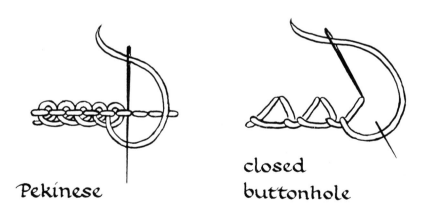

Pekinese

closed
buttonhole

GUEST TOWELS

Turn narrow hems on long sides before
neatening each end

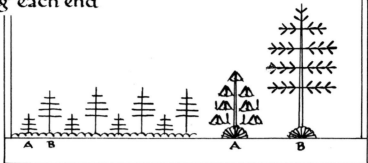

Use coton à broder or star sylko Nº 8, on
linen, fine Hardanger, or huckaback
towelling

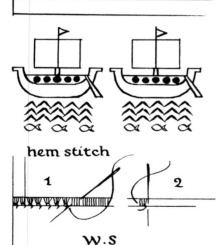

hem stitch

1   2

W.S

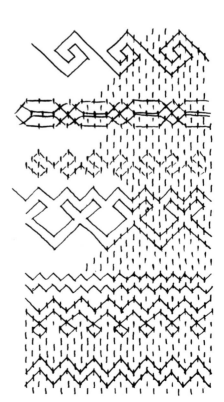

In huckaback darning
the thread must be long
because it is difficult
to join invisibly

CHAIR BACKS

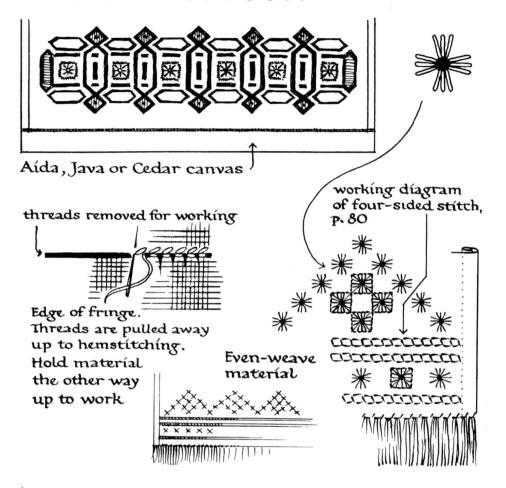

Aida, Java or Cedar canvas

threads removed for working

Edge of fringe.
Threads are pulled away
up to hemstitching.
Hold material
the other way
up to work

Even-weave
material

working diagram
of four-sided stitch,
p. 80

Use 3 ply wool for needleweaving on hessian, or
Terrazzo and Granite cloths

NEEDLEWEAVING

hem stitch into
bunches before
needleweaving

method

CUSHION

avoid finishing with a different line of pattern.⌐

Use gingham and plain cotton

The elephant can be worked in surface stitches or applied using a colour to match the gingham; edges can be left raw and covered with stitches or turned under and hemmed

When embroidery is finished the seams may be joined with insertion stitch or with a simple seam as used to sew both sides of the cushion together

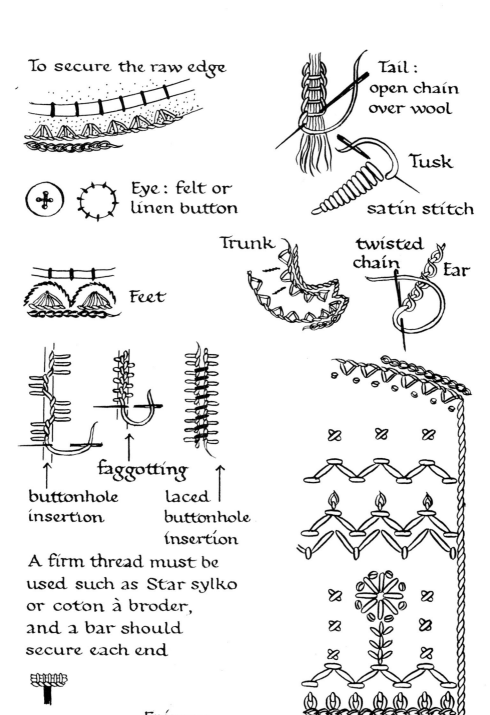

To secure the raw edge

Tail:
open chain
over wool

Tusk
satin stitch

Eye: felt or
linen button

Trunk

twisted
chain

Ear

Feet

faggotting

buttonhole
insertion

laced
buttonhole
insertion

A firm thread must be
used such as Star sylko
or coton à broder,
and a bar should
secure each end

Fringe:
Anchor soft threaded
through chain stitch

TOY

felt,
sewn with coton à broder

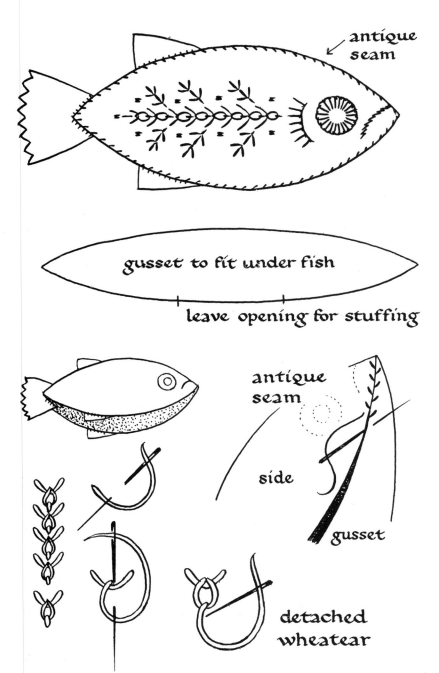

antique
seam

gusset to fit under fish

leave opening for stuffing

antique
seam

side

gusset

detached
wheatear

54

PINCUSHION

felt,
sewn with coton à broder

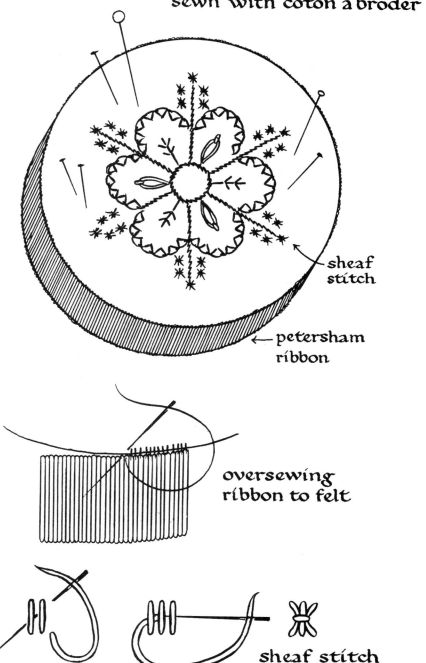

sheaf
stitch

petersham
ribbon

oversewing
ribbon to felt

sheaf stitch

55

TOYS of felt or cotton

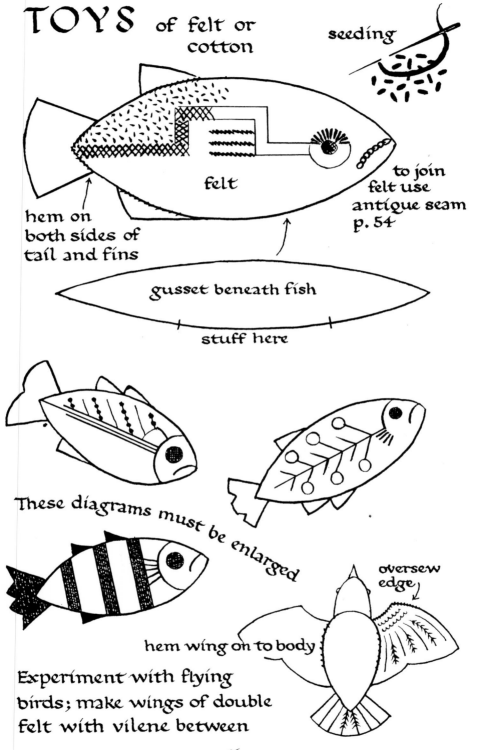

seeding

to join felt use antique seam p. 54

hem on both sides of tail and fins

felt

gusset beneath fish

stuff here

These diagrams must be enlarged

oversew edge

hem wing on to body

Experiment with flying birds; make wings of double felt with vilene between

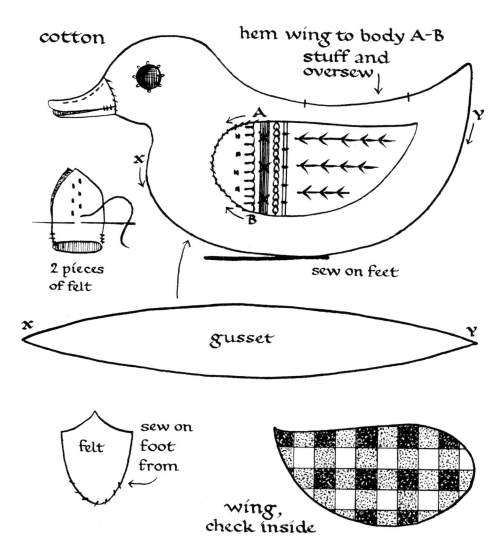

cotton

hem wing to body A-B
stuff and
oversew

A

B

x

Y

2 pieces
of felt

sew on feet

x   gusset   Y

felt

sew on
foot
from

wing,
check inside

To make up wing,
tack embroidered
and checked pieces
over vilene, place
wrong sides together;
oversew all round,
then hem A-B only

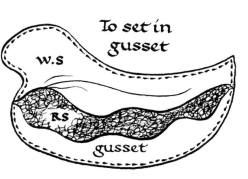

To set in
gusset

w.s

RS

gusset

APRON

to set on the waistband
see p. 41

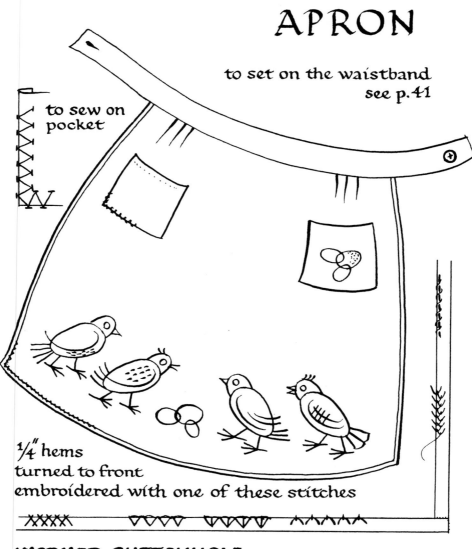

to sew on
pocket

¼" hems
turned to front
embroidered with one of these stitches

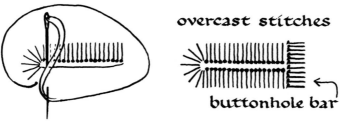

WORKED BUTTONHOLE

overcast stitches

buttonhole bar

chained
feather
stitch

Pocket — tack single turning on
3 sides; make hem on top edge

58

Template

If material is to be
applied, tack it over
a paper pattern

surface
stitches

hemmed
appliqué;
gingham

embroidered
linen buttons

hemmed
appliqué;
plain fabric

double knot stitch

59

APRON

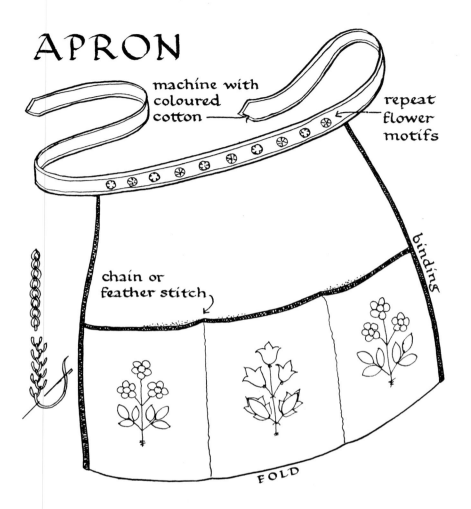

machine with coloured cotton ——

repeat flower motifs

binding

chain or feather stitch

FOLD

for needlework or gardening

use linen
use Winchester cloth
or Slavonic crash

To make the waistband —
Cut fabric twice the width of the finished band, with turnings. Fold right sides together and sew from each end leaving a space in the centre for the pinafore
To set on band see p.41

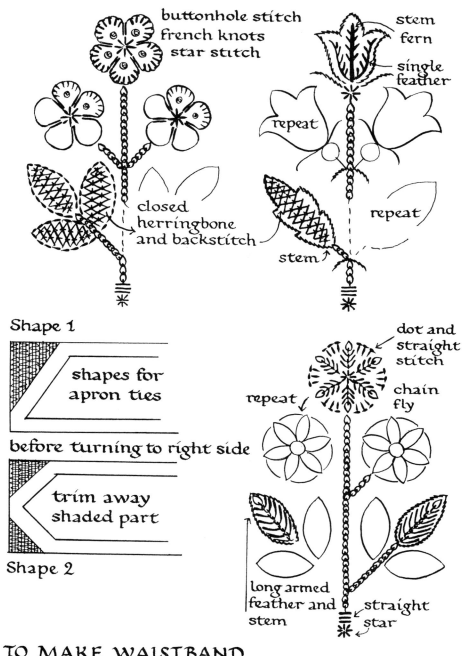

buttonhole stitch
french knots
star stitch

stem
fern

single
feather

repeat

repeat

closed
herringbone
and backstitch

stem

Shape 1

shapes for
apron ties

before turning to right side

trim away
shaded part

Shape 2

dot and
straight
stitch

chain
fly

repeat

long armed
feather and
stem

straight
star

TO MAKE WAISTBAND

FOLD

seam   space for apron   seam

ends can also be square

CHAIR PAD
patchwork with two colours

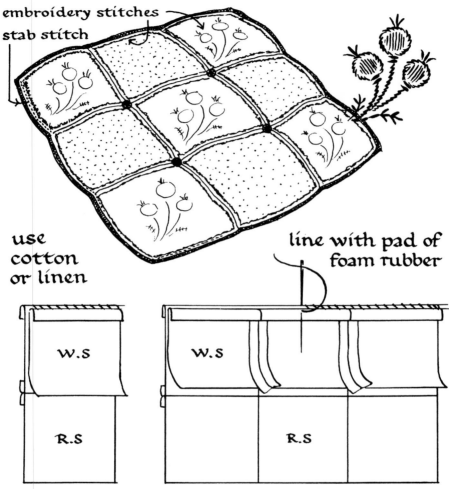

embroidery stitches
stab stitch

use
cotton
or linen

line with pad of
foam rubber

W.S

W.S

R.S

R.S

oversewing stitches must not show on the front

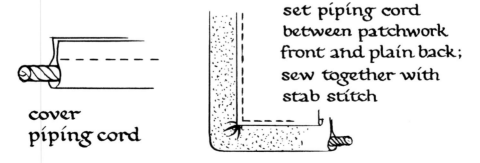

cover
piping cord

set piping cord
between patchwork
front and plain back;
sew together with
stab stitch

KETTLE HOLDER

in patchwork

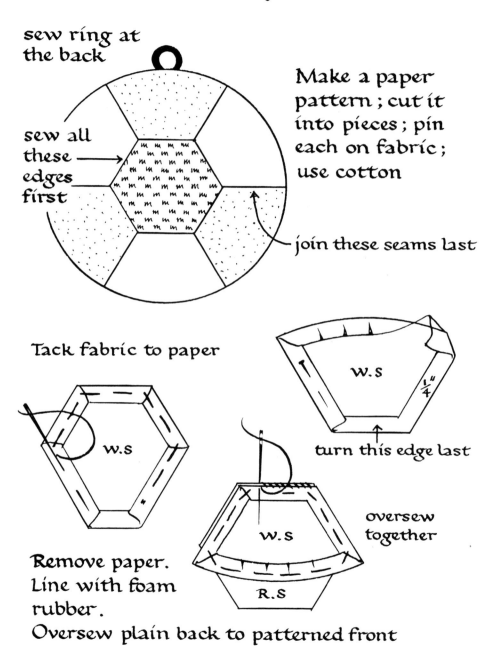

sew ring at the back

sew all these edges first

Make a paper pattern ; cut it into pieces ; pin each on fabric ; use cotton

join these seams last

Tack fabric to paper

w.s

w.s

turn this edge last

w.s

R.S

oversew together

Remove paper. Line with foam rubber.

Oversew plain back to patterned front

PADDED COT COVER

cotton interlined with blanket

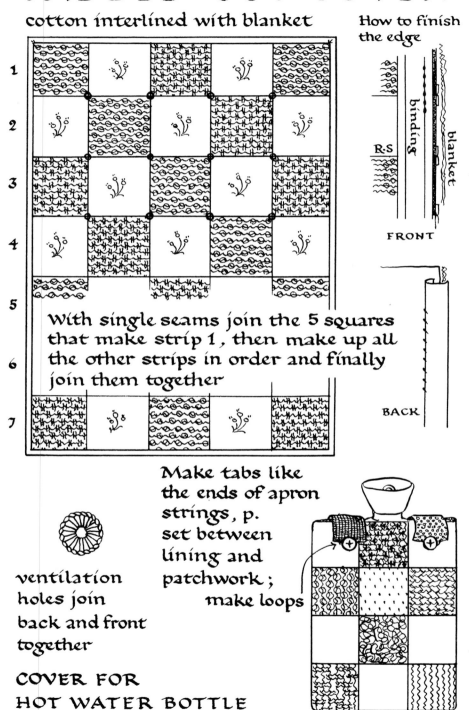

How to finish the edge

binding

R·S

blanket

FRONT

BACK

1

2

3

4

5

With single seams join the 5 squares that make strip 1, then make up all the other strips in order and finally join them together

6

7

ventilation holes join back and front together

Make tabs like the ends of apron strings, p. set between lining and patchwork; make loops

COVER FOR HOT WATER BOTTLE

CHAIR PAD
cotton or linen
patchwork in 2 colours

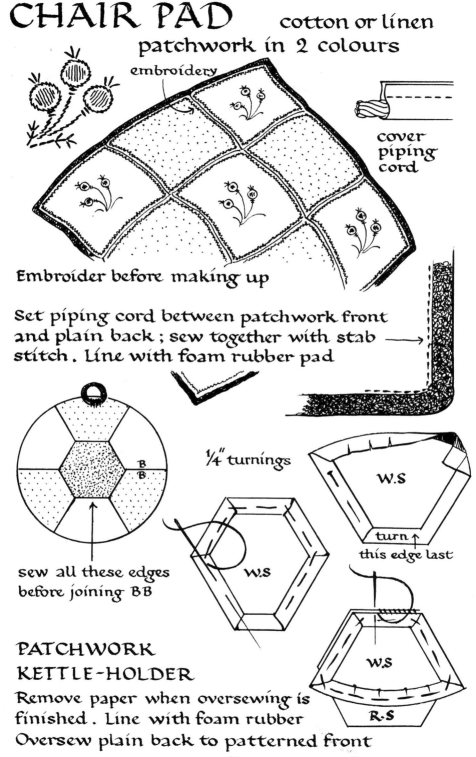

embroidery

cover
piping
cord

Embroider before making up

Set piping cord between patchwork front
and plain back; sew together with stab
stitch. Line with foam rubber pad

¼" turnings

W.S

B
B

W.S

W.S

turn ↑
this edge last

sew all these edges
before joining BB

W.S

R.S

PATCHWORK
KETTLE-HOLDER

Remove paper when oversewing is
finished. Line with foam rubber
Oversew plain back to patterned front

PINCUSHIONS

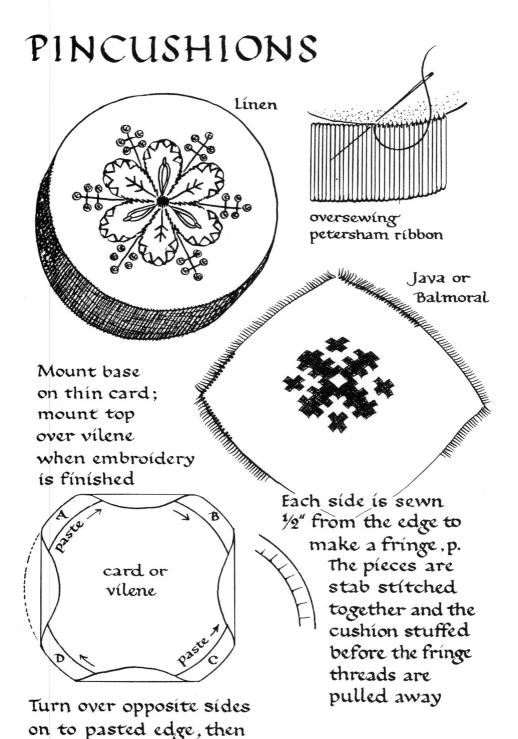

Linen

oversewing
petersham ribbon

Java or
Balmoral

Mount base
on thin card;
mount top
over vilene
when embroidery
is finished

A
paste
B

card or
vilene

paste
D
C

Turn over opposite sides
on to pasted edge, then
turn down ABCD, easing
fullness until almost flat

Each side is sewn
½" from the edge to
make a fringe, p.
The pieces are
stab stitched
together and the
cushion stuffed
before the fringe
threads are
pulled away

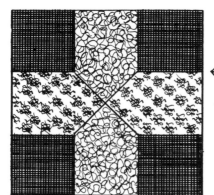

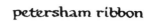
petersham ribbon

← Join top to base with ribbon

Patchwork
method
p. 65

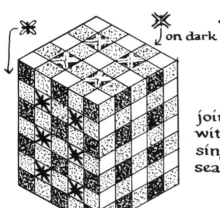

✳ ✳ on dark

join
with
single
seams

Gingham, showing how
to change its tone

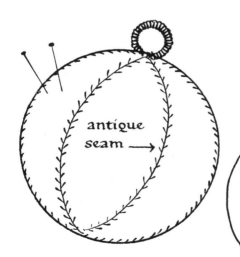

antique
seam →

Cut 6 pieces of felt

felt

even weave fabric

base stiffened
with cardboard

BAGS

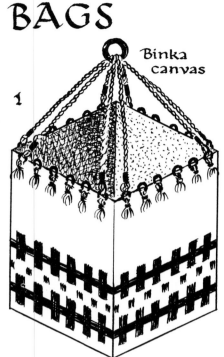

Binka canvas

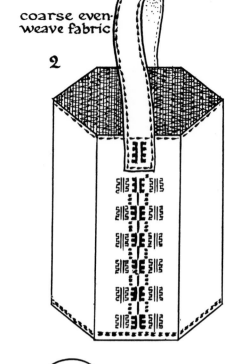

coarse even-weave fabric

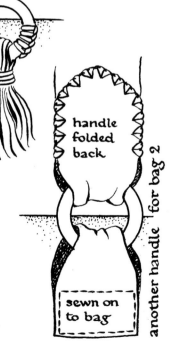

handle folded back

sewn on to bag

another handle for bag 2

Bag 1 has 4 sides, each stiffened and lined and sewn on to a square base

Bag 2 has 6 sides made in the same way, sewn on to a hexagonal base

The finished pieces can be oversewn together or joined by faggotting and oversewn to the thicker base

for SLIPPERS or KNITTING

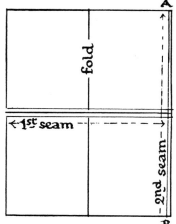

To make up, join lining and outer fabric, then fold lengthways and join A-B, again using a simple seam. Turn to the right side, turn in the bottom edges and oversew.

For the base, paste fabric on 2 pieces of card and paste them together

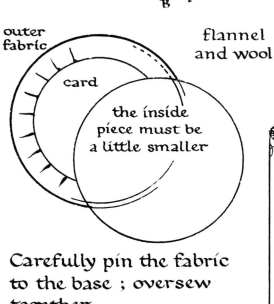

outer fabric

card

the inside piece must be a little smaller

flannel and wool

1st seam

couching

double overcast for strength

2nd seam

Carefully pin the fabric to the base ; oversew together

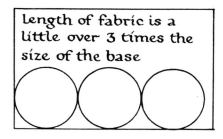

length of fabric is a little over 3 times the size of the base

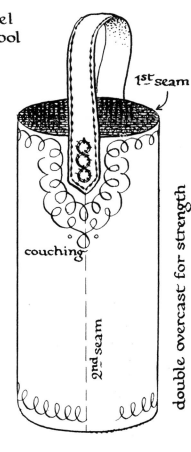

FEEDER

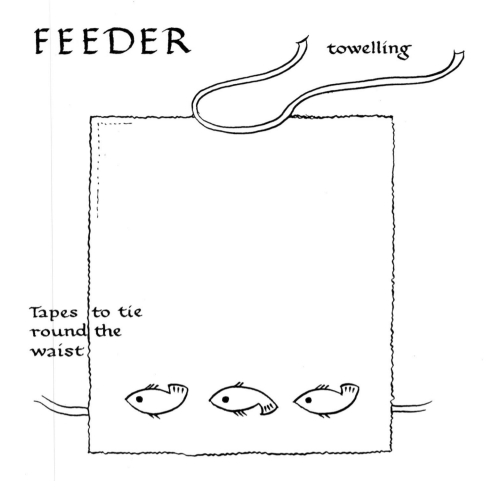

towelling

Tapes to tie round the waist

Turn double hem ; hem long sides before top and lower edges, then bind neck with tape

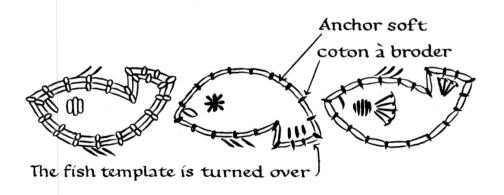

Anchor soft coton à broder

The fish template is turned over

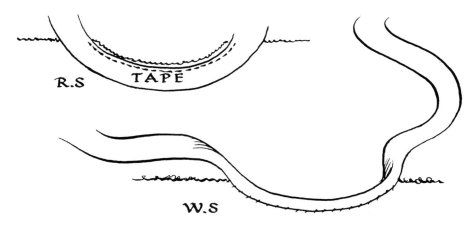

R.S   TAPE

W.S

Since the neck is very shallow it can be
bound with tape which will form 10" ties

Cut paper templates of fish or owls ; pin
on to towelling, tack just beyond edge,
remove paper and begin embroidery

FEEDER

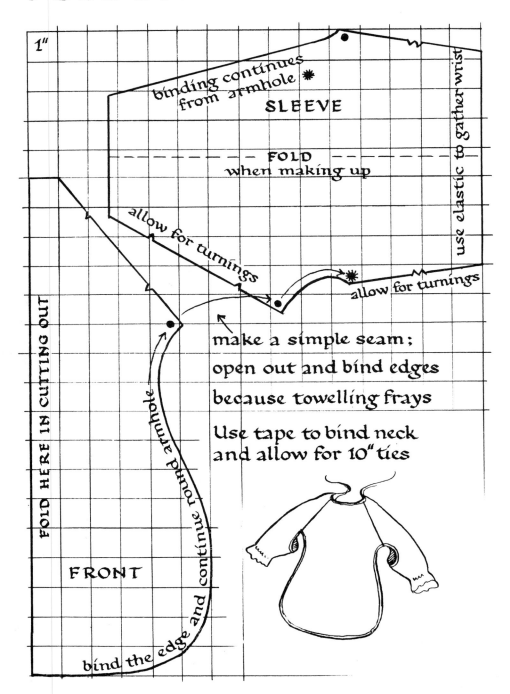

1"

binding continues
from armhole ✱

SLEEVE

FOLD
when making up

allow for turnings

use elastic to gather wrist

allow for turnings

FOLD HERE IN CUTTING OUT

continue round armhole

make a simple seam;
open out and bind edges
because towelling frays

Use tape to bind neck
and allow for 10" ties

FRONT

bind the edge and

72

FEEDER

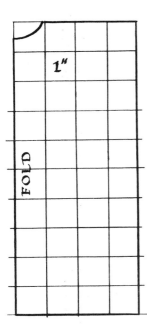

Hem long side, then bottom
edge and shoulder.
Bind neck with tape and let
this form 10" ties

Embroidery on towelling
has to be bold because detail
is hidden by the pile

Outline the fishes with
Anchor soft couching

Apply linen for the owls

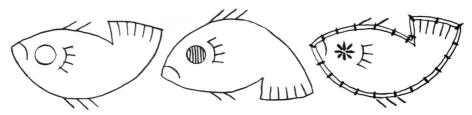

The fish template is turned over

Embroider a border of owls using a paper
template to cut shapes for hemmed appliqué

BEST BIBS

construction is the same for both bibs

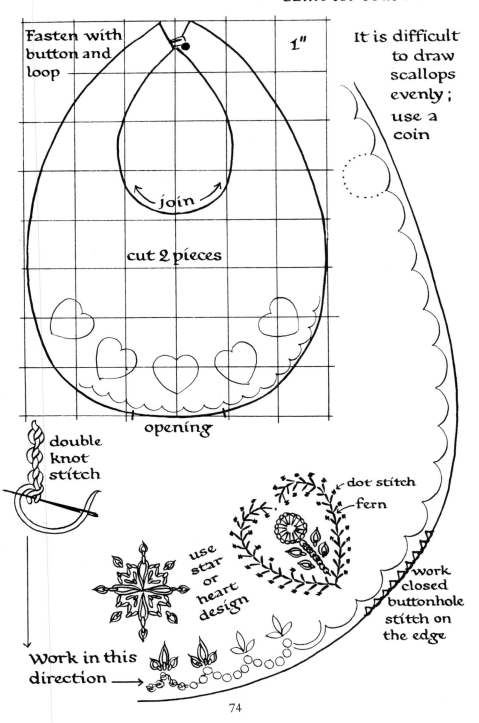

Fasten with button and loop

1"

It is difficult to draw scallops evenly; use a coin

join

cut 2 pieces

opening

double knot stitch

dot stitch

fern

use star or heart design

work closed buttonhole stitch on the edge

Work in this direction →

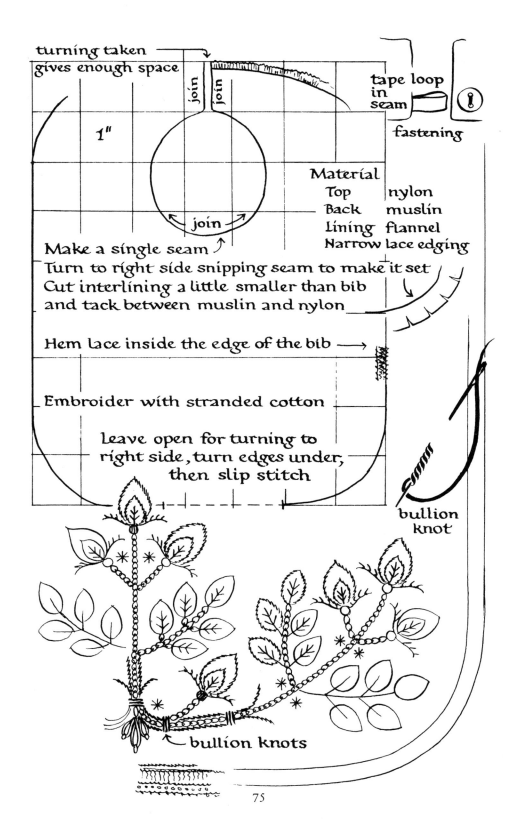

turning taken
gives enough space

join join

tape loop
in
seam

fastening

1"

join

Material
Top   nylon
Back   muslin
Lining   flannel
Narrow lace edging

Make a single seam ↗

Turn to right side snipping seam to make it set

Cut interlining a little smaller than bib
and tack between muslin and nylon

Hem lace inside the edge of the bib →

Embroider with stranded cotton

Leave open for turning to
right side, turn edges under,
then slip stitch

bullion
knot

bullion knots

TEA COSY COVER

do not cut corners

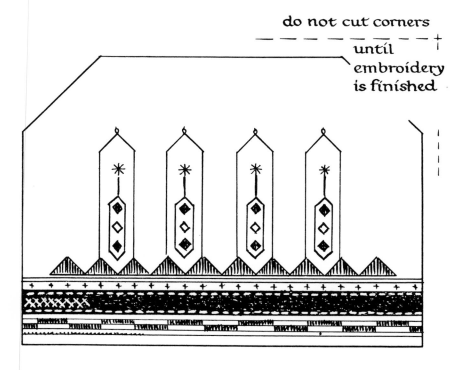

until
embroidery
is finished

Hem stitch the lower edge working from
the back

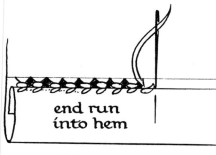

end run
into hem

When embroidery
is finished, join the
tea cosy with a
simple seam

see p. 50

Use Slavonic crash or an
even weave fabric

Work with Anchor soft
and stranded cotton

2 rows of straight
binding joined
with running
stitch beneath
the herringbone

TEA COSY COVERS

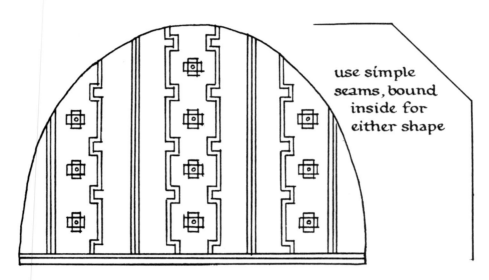

use simple
seams, bound
inside for
either shape

Counted satin stitch on even weave fabric

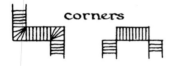

corners

The 3 or 4 sided cover on
the opposite page is made
of organdie over fine
cotton. It can be in shadow
work in double back stitch
on the wrong side, before
it is lined , or it can be
entirely in back
stitch in 2 colours,
worked through both
fabrics at once

blue

←white

blue ↓

blue ↗

↖ white

78

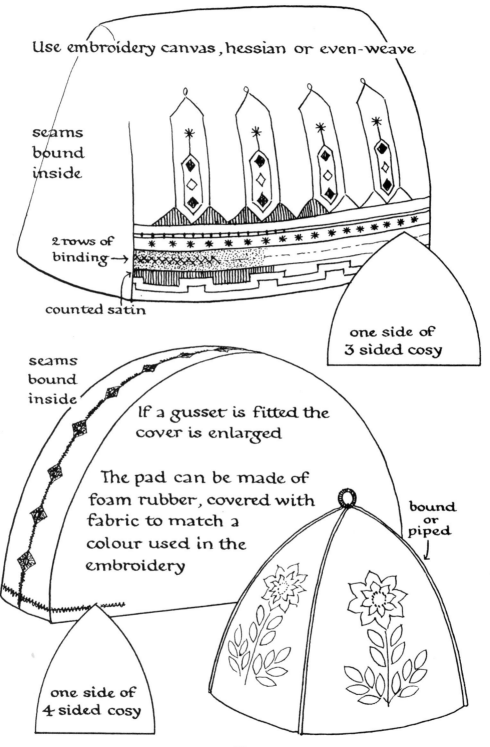

Use embroidery canvas, hessian or even-weave

seams
bound
inside

2 rows of
binding →

counted satin

one side of
3 sided cosy

seams
bound
inside

If a gusset is fitted the
cover is enlarged

The pad can be made of
foam rubber, covered with
fabric to match a
colour used in the
embroidery

bound
or
piped

one side of
4 sided cosy

79

TRAY CLOTHS

with 3 ways of finishing the edge

Use Star sylko,
coton à broder or
stranded cotton

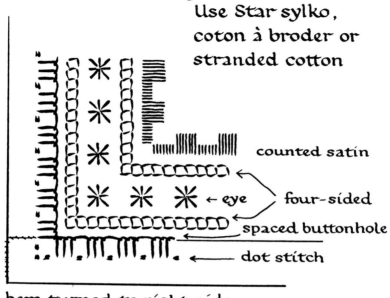

counted satin

← eye

four-sided

spaced buttonhole

dot stitch

hem turned to right side

eye stitch — each thread is
taken through
the same hole

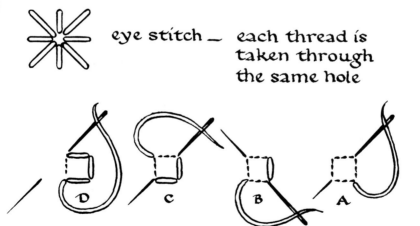

four sided stitch is worked from right to left

Use an even weave fabric
or Cedar canvas

For a
fringe :
remove
threads
after
either
4 sided stitch or
cross stitch
is complete

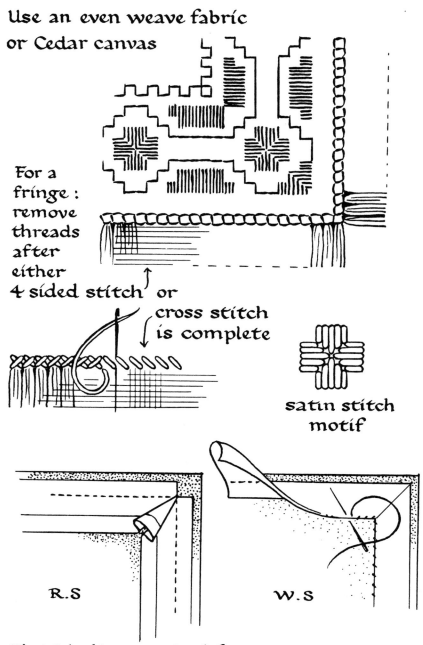

satin stitch
motif

R.S   W.S

Flat binding method for neatening an edge

TRAY CLOTHS

If heavy fabric is chosen a thick hem must
be avoided ; use one of these methods

1. Fringe the edge after hemstitching or
   working four-sided stitch
2. Turn under once ; work buttonhole stitch
3. Neaten with a bound edge
4. Neaten with flat binding at the back

threads removed when work is finished

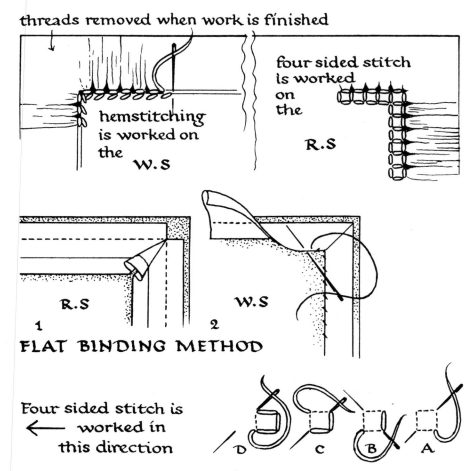

hemstitching
is worked on
the
W.S

four sided stitch
is worked
on
the
R.S

R.S
1

W.S
2

FLAT BINDING METHOD

Four sided stitch is
← worked in
this direction

D   C   B   A

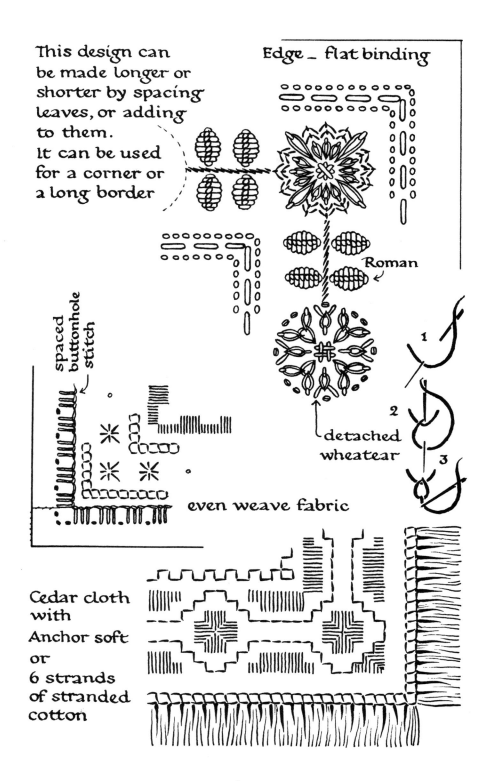

This design can
be made longer or
shorter by spacing
leaves, or adding
to them.
It can be used
for a corner or
a long border

Edge — flat binding

Roman

spaced buttonhole stitch

1

2

3

detached wheatear

even weave fabric

Cedar cloth
with
Anchor soft
or
6 strands
of stranded
cotton

83

REINS
without fastenings

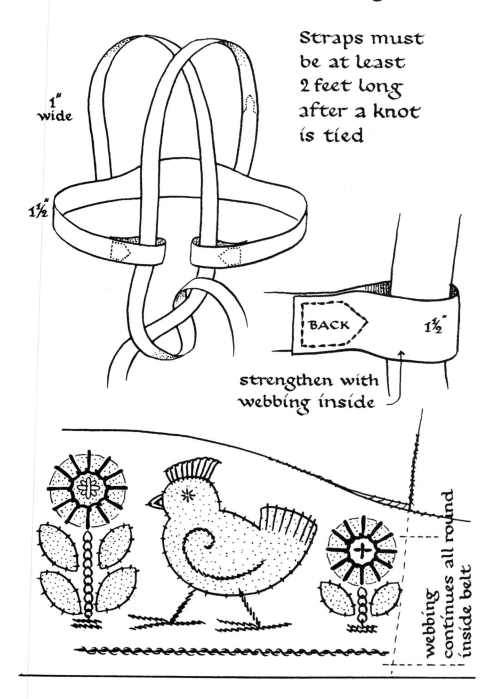

Straps must
be at least
2 feet long
after a knot
is tied

1" wide

1½"

BACK

1½"

strengthen with
webbing inside

webbing
continues all round
inside belt

84

Make straps of
2 layers of
webbing;
decorate with
embroidery
and felt

actual
size

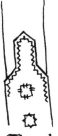

The belt is made of 2 layers of felt
lined with vilene. Straps are set
between and taken to the lower
edge for strength

$2\frac{1}{2}$"

about 6" between

CAP   felt

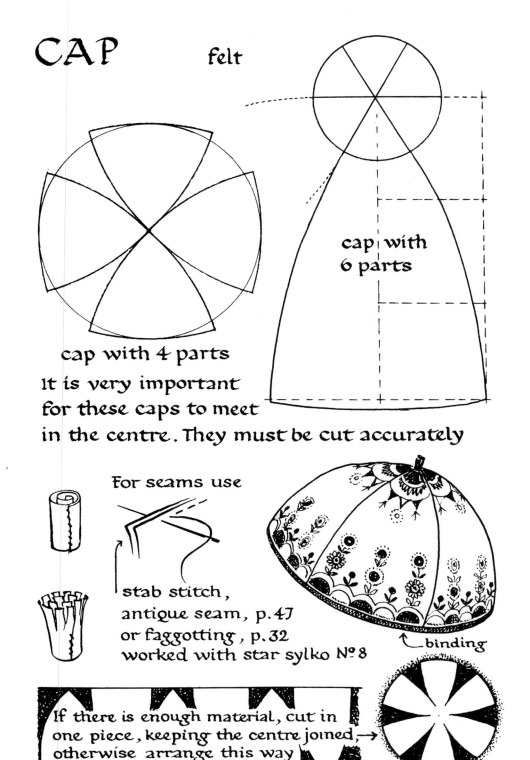

cap with 4 parts

cap with
6 parts

It is very important
for these caps to meet
in the centre. They must be cut accurately

For seams use

stab stitch,
antique seam, p.47
or faggotting, p.32
worked with star sylko № 8

binding

If there is enough material, cut in
one piece, keeping the centre joined,→
otherwise arrange this way

REINS without fastenings

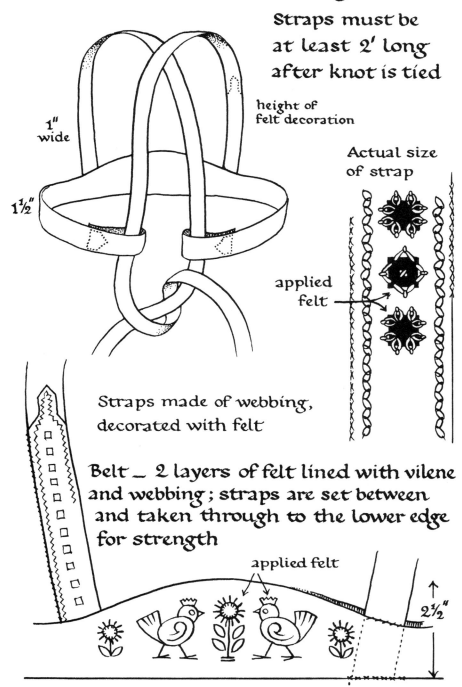

Straps must be
at least 2' long
after knot is tied

height of
felt decoration

1" wide

1½"

Actual size
of strap

applied
felt

Straps made of webbing,
decorated with felt

Belt _ 2 layers of felt lined with vilene
and webbing; straps are set between
and taken through to the lower edge
for strength

applied felt

2½"

about 6" between straps

SUMMER BONNET

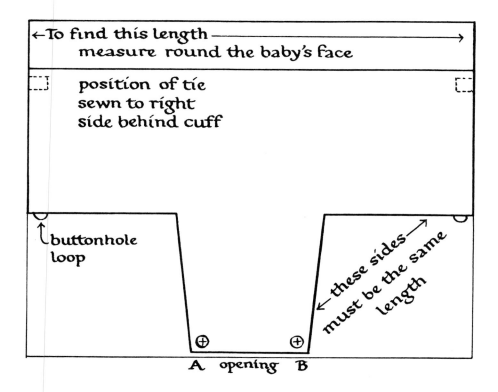

←To find this length ————————→
measure round the baby's face

position of tie
sewn to right
side behind cuff

buttonhole
loop

←these sides→
must be the same
length

A opening B

This bonnet opens flat for ironing
Cut 2 pieces of cotton fabric; join them
together all round the edges, except A-B.

Turn to right side
through A-B; close
with slip stitch

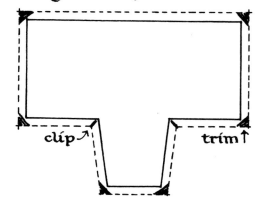

clip↗   trim↑

Trim corners and
clip to stitching

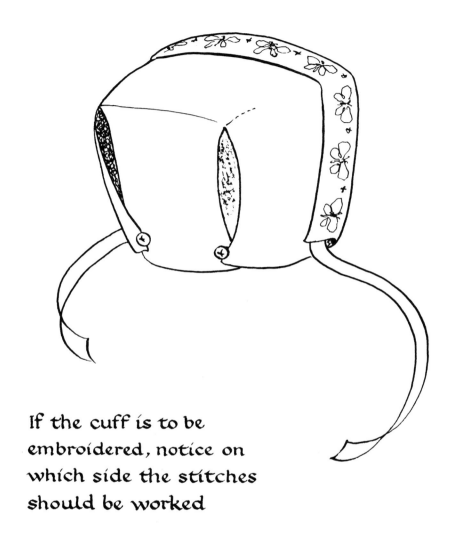

If the cuff is to be
embroidered, notice on
which side the stitches
should be worked

* * stem stitch beyond
buttonhole
makes a
stronger line

BONNET with coloured cuff

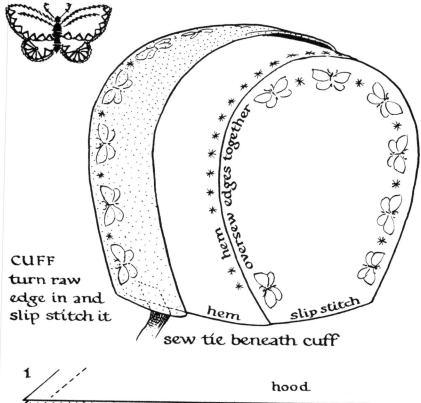

CUFF
turn raw
edge in and
slip stitch it

hem oversew edges together

hem   slip stitch

sew tie beneath cuff

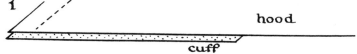

1   hood
cuff

2   cuff
     hood

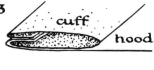

3   cuff
     hood

Make back of double fabric,
turn to right side and slip
stitch bottom edge.
Pin curve to hood, from
centre outwards, easing
straight edge to curve.
Oversew together

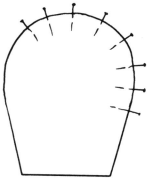

SUMMER BONNET

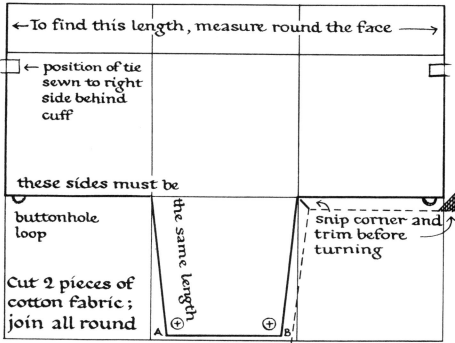

←To find this length, measure round the face →

← position of tie sewn to right side behind cuff

these sides must be

buttonhole loop

the same length

snip corner and trim before turning

Cut 2 pieces of cotton fabric; join all round

A ⊕   ⊕ B

except between A-B; turn to the right side through this opening; slip stitch together

This bonnet opens flat for ironing

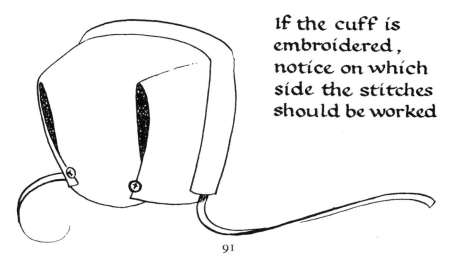

If the cuff is embroidered, notice on which side the stitches should be worked

BAG organdie or spotted muslin

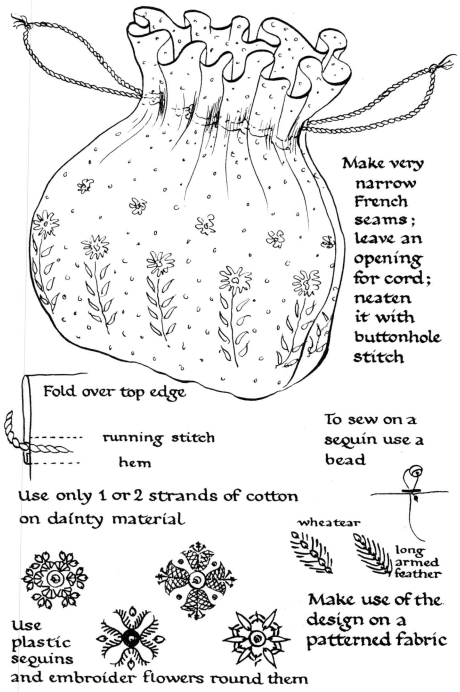

Make very
narrow
French
seams;
leave an
opening
for cord;
neaten
it with
buttonhole
stitch

Fold over top edge

running stitch

hem

To sew on a
sequin use a
bead

Use only 1 or 2 strands of cotton
on dainty material

wheatear

long
armed
feather

Make use of the
design on a
patterned fabric

Use
plastic
sequins
and embroider flowers round them

92

KNITTING BAG

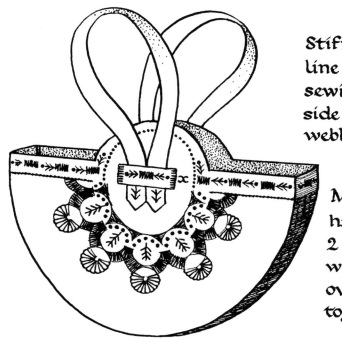

Stiffen and line before sewing each side to narrow webbing

Make the handles of 2 pieces of webbing oversewn together

Apply a strap, x, across the handles, for strength

To arrange the design, cut out paper templates and tack round them

Bind raw edges inside the bag

Use wool on hessian or other heavy fabric

HOW TO NEATEN A SEAM WITH BIAS BINDING

stitch right sides together, turn bias binding over seam, hem into stitches

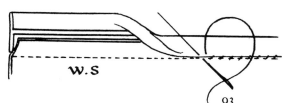

w.s

PATCHWORK BEACH BAG

to lie on when it is open flat

Linen or cotton

Make paper pattern as diagram. Cut up pattern and place pieces on the fabric; allow ½" turnings. Tack paper and fabric together. Oversew. Begin in the centre

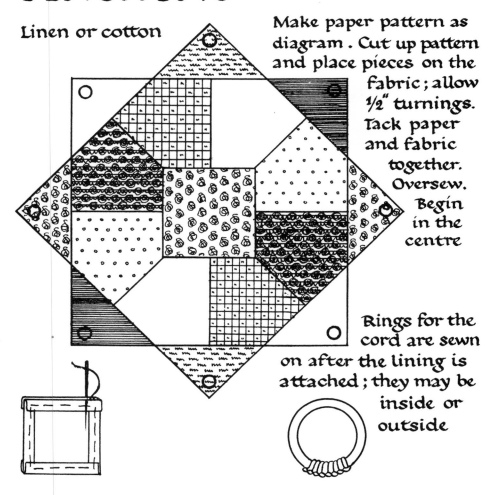

Rings for the cord are sewn on after the lining is attached; they may be inside or outside

Cut plastic lining; place right sides together; join with simple seam; leave one ∨ open; remove paper and turn through opening; close with slip stitch, running the needle between the two edges of material with invisible stitches

HOW TO MAKE A TWISTED CORD

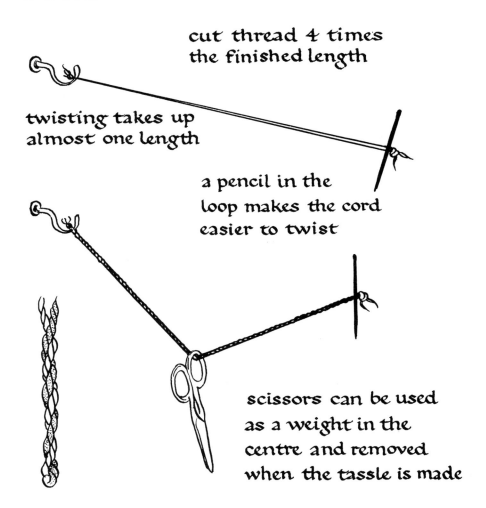

cut thread 4 times
the finished length

twisting takes up
almost one length

a pencil in the
loop makes the cord
easier to twist

scissors can be used
as a weight in the
centre and removed
when the tassle is made

Cut several pieces of thread 4 times the
finished length ; knot each end ; twist
very tightly and bring the ends together
keeping taut all the time. The cord will
twist naturally

HARDANGER MAT

Use double even weave, Hardanger type fabric

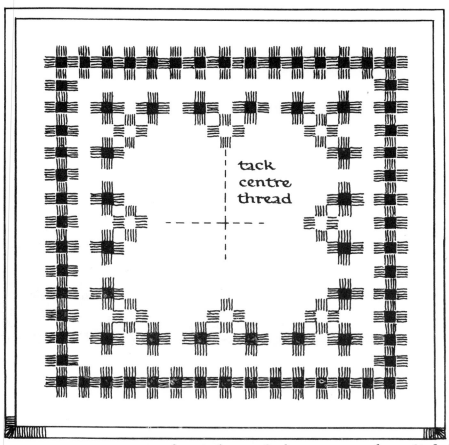

tack
centre
thread

edge trimmed close to satin stitch

In Hardanger work a hole
may be cut only if the raw
edge is covered with satin
stitch

Work 5 stitches over 4 threads

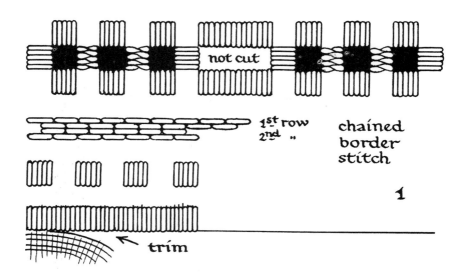

not cut

1st row
2nd "

chained
border
stitch

1

trim

Plan these borders on drafting paper

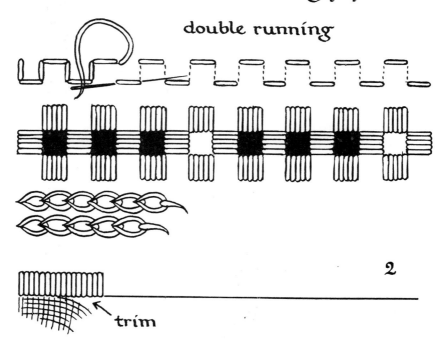

double running

2

trim

TWO ALTERNATIVE BORDER PATTERNS

HARDANGER WORK

Make a design from these units. There are
5 satin stitches over 4 cut threads

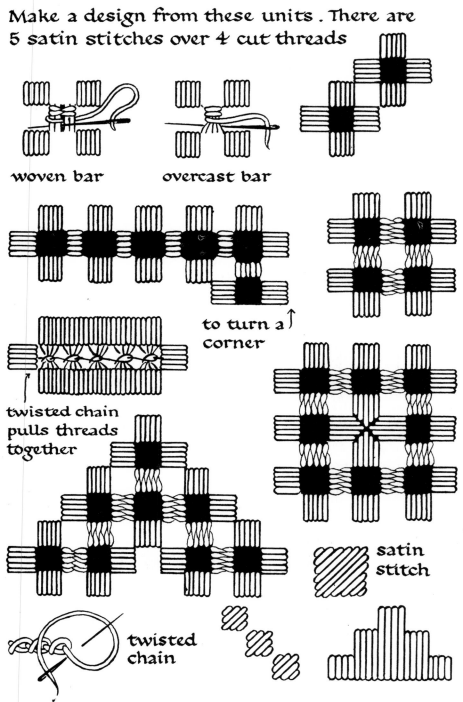

woven bar

overcast bar

to turn a↑
corner

twisted chain
pulls threads
together

satin
stitch

twisted
chain

for MATS and CUSHIONS

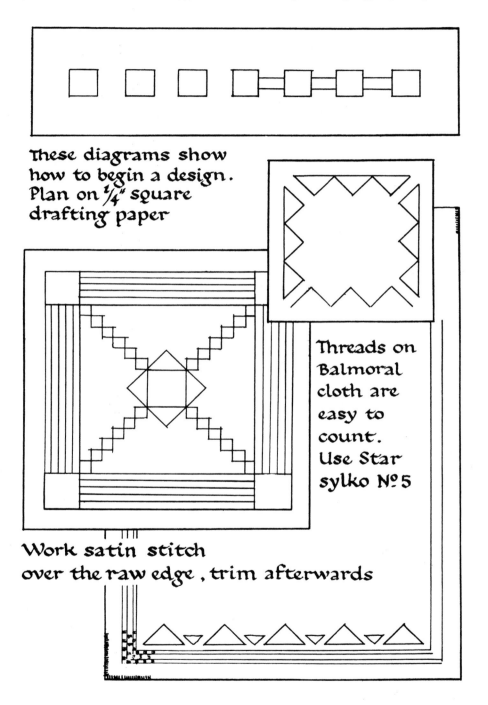

These diagrams show
how to begin a design.
Plan on ¼" square
drafting paper

Threads on
Balmoral
cloth are
easy to
count.
Use Star
sylko Nº 5

Work satin stitch
over the raw edge, trim afterwards

CUSHIONS

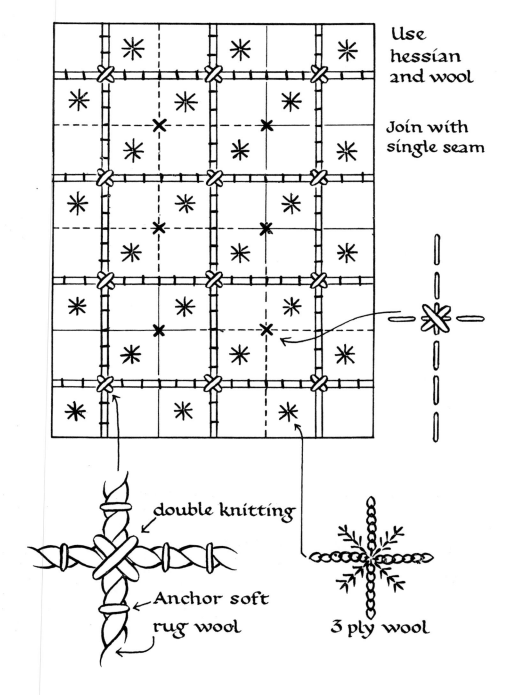

Use
hessian
and wool

Join with
single seam

double knitting

Anchor soft
rug wool

3 ply wool

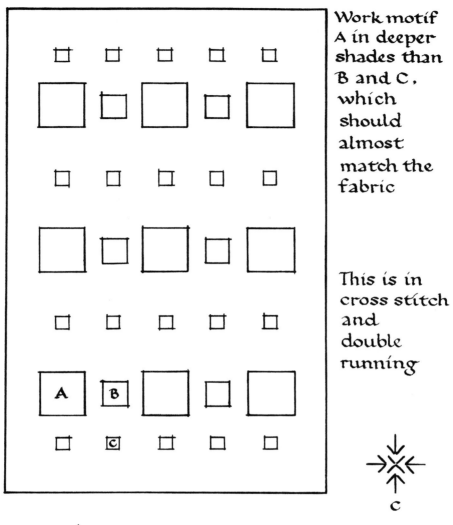

Work motif
A in deeper
shades than
B and C,
which
should
almost
match the
fabric

This is in
cross stitch
and
double
running

C

A

B

Use even-weave fabric

CUSHIONS

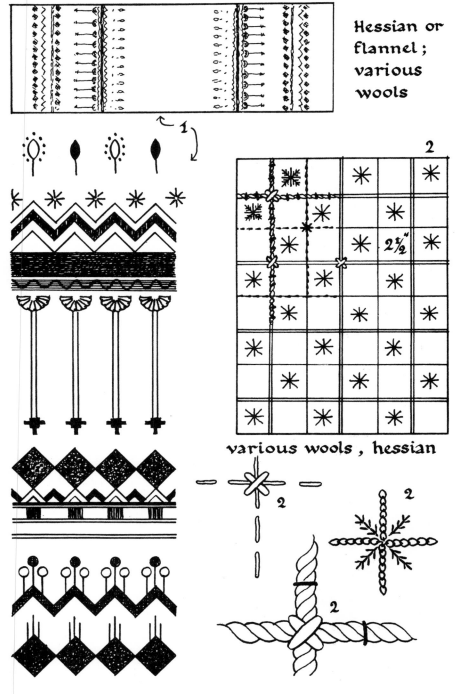

Hessian or flannel; various wools

1

2

2½"

various wools, hessian

2

2

2

102

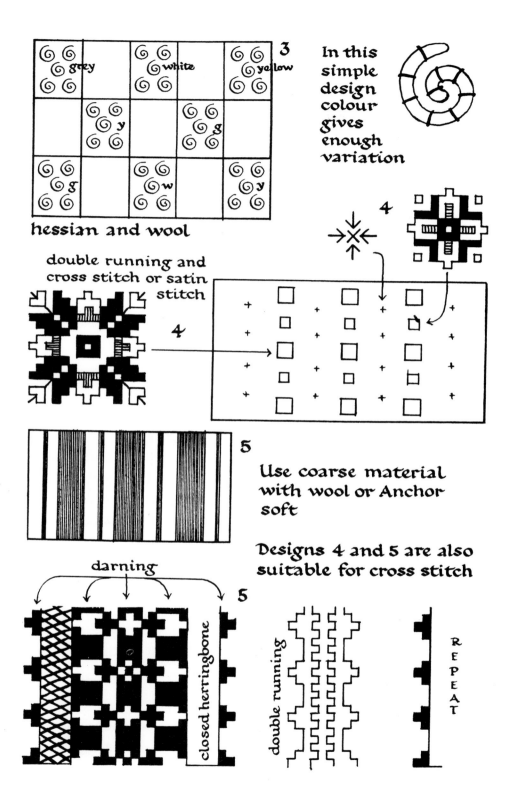

3

grey white yellow

y g

g w y

In this
simple
design
colour
gives
enough
variation

hessian and wool

double running and
cross stitch or satin
stitch

4

4

Use coarse material
with wool or Anchor
soft

Designs 4 and 5 are also
suitable for cross stitch

5

5

darning

closed herringbone

double running

REPEAT

BABY SHOES
cotton

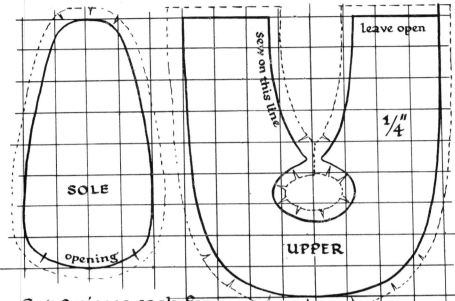

SOLE

opening

leave open

Sew on this line

¼"

UPPER

Cut 2 pieces each for
sole and upper ; remember to plan for 2 shoes.

Join together both pieces of
sole and of upper. Pin and
tack one side over wadding;
carefully turn to right side,
snipping to help a smooth
turn. Slip stitch sole at
toe, and upper at heel.
Oversew heel seam and
upper to sole, easing in
fullness at toe.
Sew on ribbons.

Embroider, securing ends in
thickness of wadding

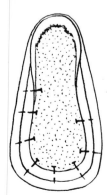

PILLOW COVER

shadow work on fine lawn or organdie

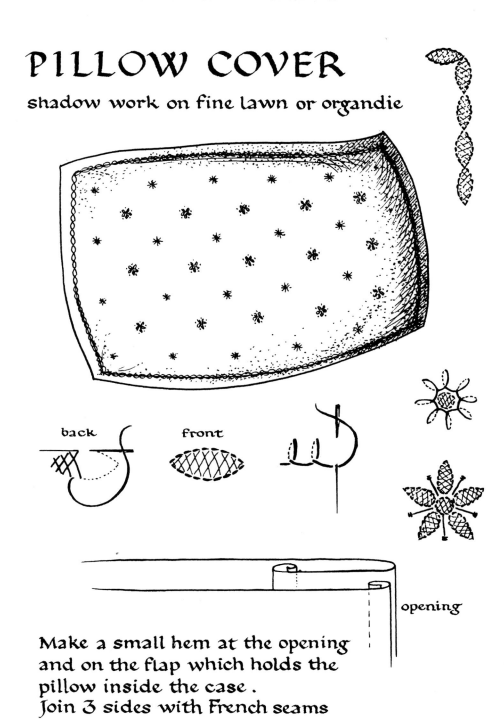

back

front

opening

Make a small hem at the opening
and on the flap which holds the
pillow inside the case.
Join 3 sides with French seams

BABY'S MITTEN

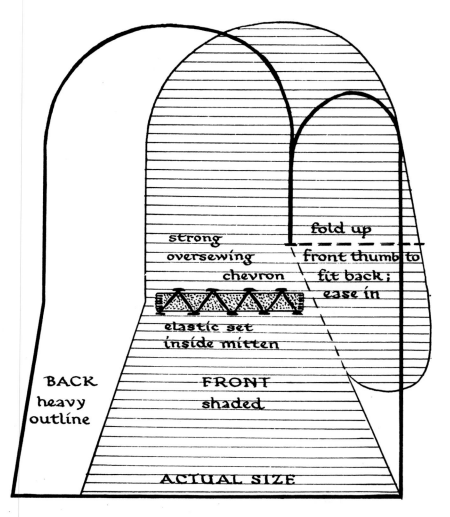

If thick non-fraying material is chosen,
seams can be joined on the outside by double
overcast, buttonhole stitch or antique seam;
hem or buttonhole the free edges

MITTEN

Coal or oven-glove without embroidery
Use closely woven woollen fabric

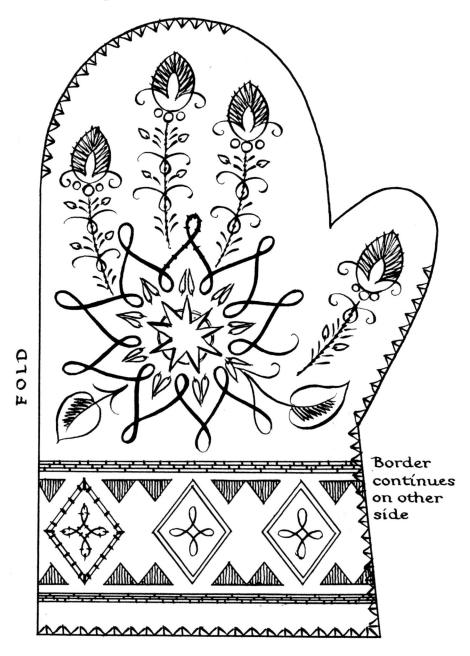

FOLD

Border
continues
on other
side

PANEL to hang,
frame, or mount as a finger plate

Hem the sides or
use hem-stitch
if working on
suitable fabric

Mount over
dowelling

This work will
look better if it is
lined, and then
interlined with
vilene

Embroider with
different types of
thread for variety

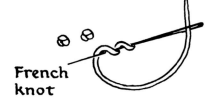

French
knot

OVEN CLOTH

Use 2 thicknesses
of honeycomb
towelling

edges bound
all round

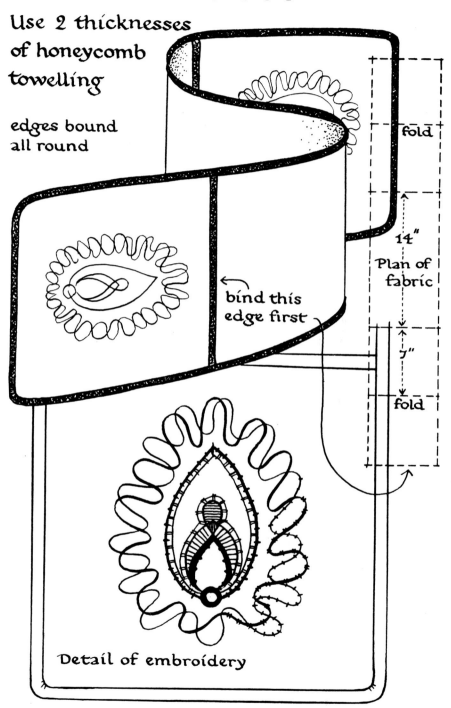

fold

← bind this
edge first

14"

Plan of
fabric

7"

fold

Detail of embroidery

MATINEE COAT

Viyella, Clydella, cotton,
brushed rayon

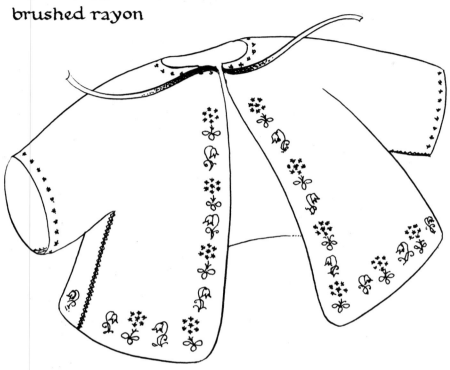

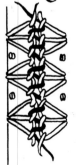

seam
enlarged

If the coat is to be lined, cut
2 identical pieces, machine
them together, leaving A~B
open to turn through; slip
stitch this together, then
work the seams

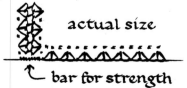

actual size

bar for strength

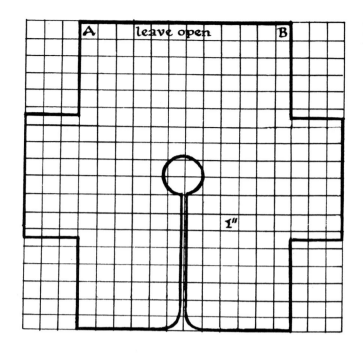

A | leave open | B

1"

❋ ❋ ❋ ❋ for neck and sleeves

work flowers before
the coat is lined

long
armed
feather

III

APRON with bib

Use linen or cotton

Set skirt into waistband as on p.41
Make ½" hem all round bib ; oversew bib to
waistband . Make each strap by machining
together on the right side, 2 pieces of turned
in fabric

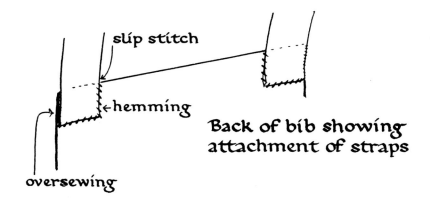

slip stitch

←hemming

oversewing

Back of bib showing attachment of straps

The body is made of striped fabric, applied and embroidered

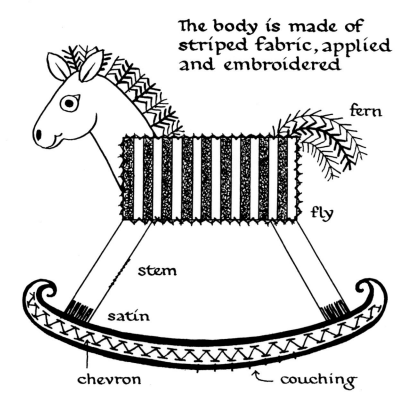

fern

fly

stem

satin

chevron

couching

LOOSE BODICE age 3-4

to wear with shorts
Cotton

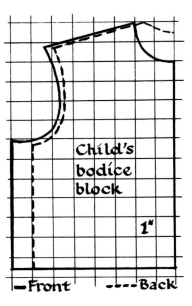

Child's bodice block

1"

Front ----Back

Adapt to design
and to fit the child;
add turnings

Edges bound to
match embroidery

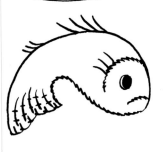

TODDLER'S SUN TOP

Cotton or towelling . It could also be used as a feeder

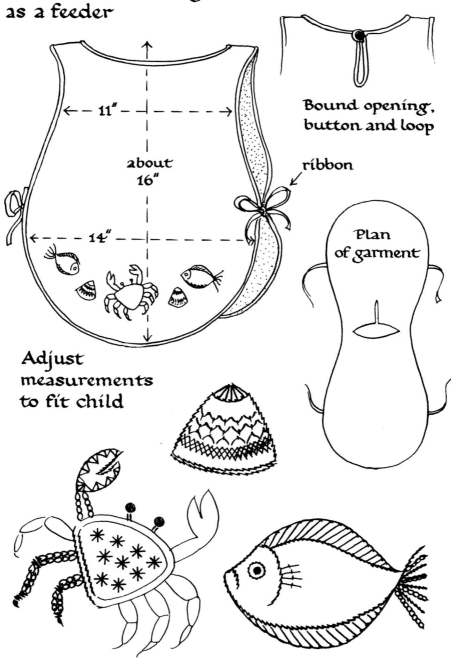

11"

about 16"

14"

Bound opening, button and loop

ribbon

Plan of garment

Adjust measurements to fit child

TODDLER'S DRESS

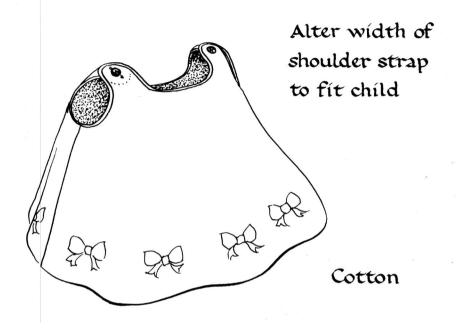

Alter width of
shoulder strap
to fit child

Cotton

Make up side seams.
One piece of binding continues round
neck and armholes

The hem can be turned up and hemmed,
bound as the neck, or finished

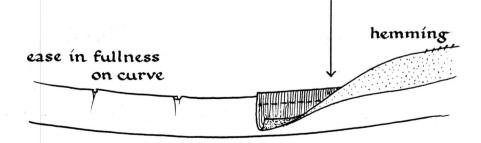

ease in fullness
on curve

hemming

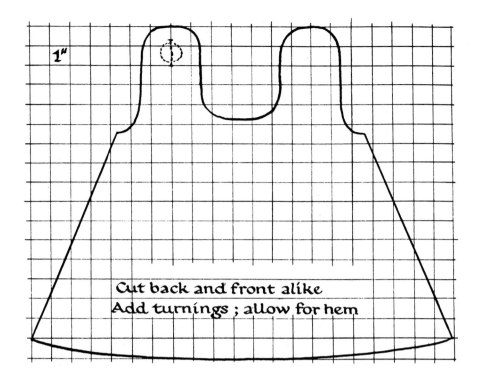

1"

Cut back and front alike
Add turnings ; allow for hem

Make a buttonhole in each front strap
Sew buttons on back straps

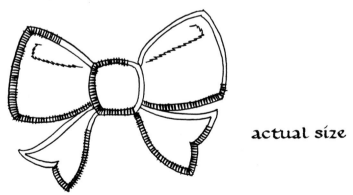

actual size

Appliqué bow sewn down with small
buttonhole stitch or overcast

NIGHTDRESS

Viyella,
plissé,
cotton

Leave seam open if a
larger armhole required;
neaten with bias binding

Decorate yoke with feather stitch

shell edging

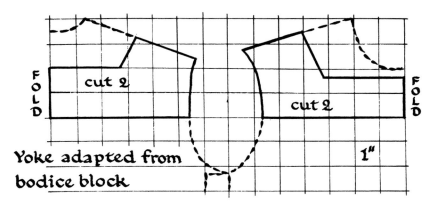

Yoke adapted from
bodice block

Cut 2 pieces of each. Join shoulder seams
of lining and outer material. Place both
together, press seams flat, join seams at
neck and armhole, diagram, turn to right
side. Crease edges of yoke, tack and set
gathers between, see apron band p. 41

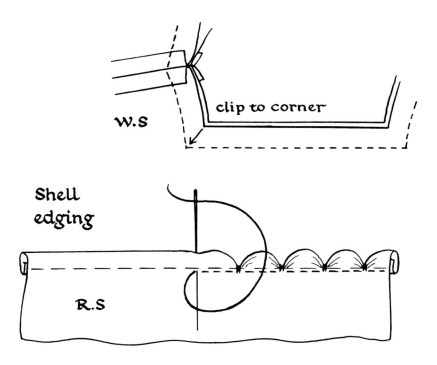

W.S

clip to corner

Shell
edging

R.S

FABRICS

LBC = Leighton, Baldwin Cox & Co. Ltd.
D = Dryads
A = Arnolds
NH = Nottingham Handicrafts

Canvas

Made by or obtainable from

patterned weave	Sumatra	36″	NH
	Java	28″	NH, LBC, A
very coarse	Aida	42″	NH, LBC, A
	Conway	42″	A
	Wharfedale	42″	A
	Binka		Penelope
finer weave	Rowan	45″	⎫
	Beech	42″	⎬ D
	Linden	42″	⎭
	Cedar	28″	

Heavy Fabric

Hessian type, coarse	Hessian	50″	various sources
	Terazzo	48″	A
	Granite	18″	A, NH
	Oatmeal	36″ 50″	NH, D
fairly coarse	Slavonic	17″ 23″	A, LBC, NH
	Winchester	42″	LBC

Hardanger type

double even weave	Hardanger	33″ 42″	LBC, D, NH
	Pine Hardanger	41″	D
	Windsor	42″	⎫ A
	Balmoral	42″	⎭
	Westminster	52″	LBC
single even weave	Willow cross stitch	52″	⎫ D
	Coarse Willow	50″	⎭
	Holyrood	54″	A
	Hereford	31″	⎫ LBC
	Canterbury	54″	⎭

Linen	Glenshee fabrics	various	} various suppliers
	Moygashel	36″	
	Old bleach	various	
	Check even weave		NH
	Huckaback towelling	18″ 22″	A

Imitation Linen	Azlin		LBC, NH
	Empire		LBC
	Larne		A

Cotton	Poplin		
	Cambric	36″	
	Lawn	41″	
	Organdie	44″	
	Gingham		
	Muslin		
	Winceyette	36″	
	Denim	36″	
	Oregon cloth	36″	D
	Bungalow cloth	42″	} NH
	Double check	42″	
	Chequer	31″	

Woollen	Flannel	
	Viyella	
	Clydella (part wool)	36″

Various Fabrics	Terry towelling	
	Honeycomb towelling	12″ 22″ 42″ A, NH
	Rayon, spun, brushed	
	Felt	
	Domette	

Other Materials	Vilene
	Patterned plastics
	Wadding
	Webbing
	Petersham ribbon
	Cord
	Ricrac
	Tape
	Foam rubber

Bibliography

Butler, Anne, *The Batsford Encyclopaedia of Embroidery Stitches*, Batsford 1979, paperback 1983

Christie, Mrs Archibald, *Samplers and Stitches*, Batsford 1920, paperback 1985

Clabburn, Pamela, *The Needleworker's Dictionary*, Macmillan 1976

Gostelow, Mary, *The Cross Stitch Book*, Batsford 1982

Gray, Jennifer, *Canvas Work*, Batsford 1974

Howard, Constance, *The Constance Howard Book of Stitches*, Batsford 1979

Howard, Constance, *Inspiration for Embroidery*, Batsford 1966, paperback 1985

Jones, Diana, *Patterns for Canvas Embroidery*, Batsford 1977, paperback 1983

Jones, Nora, *Embroidery* (Guidelines series), Macdonald Educational 1978

Morrell, Anne, *Stitchery* (leaflet) Embroiderers' Guild 1983

Morrell, Anne, *Using Simple Embroidery Stitches*, Batsford 1985

100 Embroidery Stitches, J & P Coats, 1967

Phillpot, Pat, *The Craft of Embroidery*, Stanley Paul 1976

Pyman, Kit (editor), *Needlecraft Series*, nos 1–16, Search Press 1979–82

Snook, Barbara, *Embroidery Stitches*, Batsford 1963

Thomas, Mary, *A Dictionary of Embroidery Stitches*, Hodder and Stoughton 1934

Index

EMBROIDERY STITCHES

THINGS TO MAKE

PROCESSES